Oct 2008

John —
Your talents & the way
you apply them are
a true example of I owe
Quadrant Thinking. I am
grateful to know you!

Tony

What Others Are Saying About
Say Hello to the Elephants

"Elephants in our closets BE GONE! These are powerful, personally compelling strategies for attacking (and overcoming) challenges with the same passion that drives us all to success."
> — Jennifer Kushell, author of the *New York Times* bestseller
> *Secrets of the Young & Successful*

"*Say Hello to the Elephants* delivers the kind of personal connection you want from every professional."
> — Keith Ferrazzi, author of *Never Eat Alone*

"The famous management expert Steven M. R. Covey advises people to 'talk straight.' Say what you mean, and don't beat around the bush! Tony Rose demonstrates how to do just that. Address the elephants and increase your confidence."
> — L. Gary Boomer, CPA, CITP, CEO of Boomer Consulting, Inc.

"Punctuated with wit and revelation."
> — Philip X. Tirone, author of *7 Steps to a 720 Credit Score*

"This book will represent a turning point in your life!"
> — Curtis Estes, author of *Your Life by Design*

"Engaging, riveting, and a must-read for anyone."
> —Eric W. Swenson, *Managing People in the 21st Century*

"Simply put, *Say Hello to the Elephants* is an essential primer on the structure of success. Tony Rose knows a lot about creating and sustaining success—he has built a highly successful, nationally recognized accounting firm, and over the past thirty years his advice and planning have been instrumental in creating hundreds of millions of dollars in additional wealth for businesses and families. This book will show you what's needed to recognize, confront, and masterfully handle your biggest issues, threats, and opportunities. The section on attaining clarity about objectives and obstacles is worth at least one hundred times the price of the book!"

— Larry Pinci and Phil Glosserman, authors of *Sell the Feeling: The 6-Step System that Drives People to Do Business with You*

"Tony Rose puts his finger on an essential truth: Even the most successful Americans find it difficult to face the issues that will make their futures enjoyable and significant. *Say Hello to the Elephants* makes the tough issues stimulating and the crucial actions satisfying."

—Dan Sullivan, founder of Strategic Coach®

SAY
HELLO
TO THE ELEPHANTS

A FOUR-PART PROCESS FOR FINDING CLARITY,
CONFRONTING PROBLEMS, AND MOVING ON

SAY
HELLO
TO THE ELEPHANTS

TONY ROSE

Edited by Jocelyn Baker

RSJ/SWENSON LLC

LOS ANGELES, CA

DEDICATION

To my wife, Chris, and my children, Jon and Katie:
Thank you for understanding that in my quest to make the lives
of my clients easier, I sometimes make your lives harder.

And to Mary Snyder, who started me down the road, and
Scott Fithian, who made sure I turned toward intentional planning:
You have passed in body, but you are present every day in spirit.

CONTENTS

Acknowledgments

THE OTHER DAY, I had a novel idea: *There **are** no new ideas!*

Since my revelation, I have decided that if there is a new idea, it is that a corollary exists to the idea that nothing is new: as the collective education of society progresses, there **are** new takes on ancient wisdom.

In other words, there are no new ideas, but there are new applications of old wisdom. I have been fortunate to learn from some of the best business thinkers and wealth counselors in the world, many of whom have tweaked conventional wisdom to apply to today's environment. I have combined their wisdom with more than thirty years' experience as a tax and business strategy advisor, and throughout the years, I have been blessed with loyal clients who appreciate these new perspectives on old wisdom.

For this gift, I am specifically indebted to Brad Spencer, PhD, Kathy Kolbe, Dan Sullivan, and the late Scott Fithian, all of whom set my course toward clarity and gave me the critical tools I use every day. Todd Fithian, Scott's brother, taught me in real-time the value of sustainability as a discipline. Karen Kass, PhD, and Mike Berlin, PhD, inspired the realization that only by understanding people can one feel passionately about accounting and tax. I am grateful to brilliant authors such as Daniel Pink, author of *A Whole New Mind*; David Maister, Charles Green, and Robert Galford, authors of *The Trusted Advisor*; W. Chan Kim and Renée Mauborgne, authors of *Blue Ocean Strategy*; the Heath brothers, Chip and Dan, authors of *Made to Stick*; and countless others who have shaped my attitude, the direction of my business, and the way I counsel my clients and address my elephants, including the members of K2, an advanced study group at the Legacy Group.

The team at Rose, Snyder & Jacobs is a constant reminder to passionately implement and sustain solutions that address our clients' overarching dreams. My partners have always supported my efforts to have our firm be just a little different. From my original partners, Greg Snyder and Jake Jacobs, I learned many of the methods presented herein, which Greg and Jake apply intuitively. My partner, Rebecca Maggard, has been a true collaborator in this endeavor and practices the "soft issue" side of accounting better than anyone I know. And our team members willingly engage in a laboratory in which we apply a variety of different solutions so that our clients have a forum to reach clarity and implement their greatest life pursuits.

A big debt of gratitude goes to Curtis Estes, author of *Your Life by Design* and a good friend, for pointing out that I should put my thoughts on paper. Jocelyn Baker, the thinking man's writer, is chiefly responsible that those thoughts actually made their way to paper. Our partner in RSJ/Swenson, Eric Swenson, gave freely of his time in reading this book and making useful suggestions on its improvements. His book, *Managing in the 21st Century*, is a critical management-training book for Rose, Snyder & Jacobs.

Say Hello to the Elephants describes the approaches that I have used with my clients and in my business over the past decade to identify opportunities, resolve conflicts, and achieve goals. During this time, my clients and I have realized tremendous growth and prosperity by applying these approaches to different life and business scenarios. A special thanks to these clients!

The Elephants in the Room

I walked through the front door of my office last week to find three of my elephants.

There they were, the elephants in the room: problems I didn't want to confront, problems I didn't know how to confront, and problems that seemed too big to tackle.

Sitting in front of my office was the first elephant: a hardworking, loyal employee who was more eager than skilled. I hoped to coach him to greatness but was afraid of the reality. If he failed to improve his job skills, I needed to terminate his employment. The situation required a difficult conversation, one I did not want to initiate.

Down the hall sat the second elephant. I am fortunate to work with people who are also my dear friends, but a professional conflict with one of them threatened the health of our business. Rather than address the situation head on, we tiptoed around each other and avoided confrontation. It just seemed easier.

My assistant greeted me. "Delores Hickey called. She is expecting a return call ASAP."

Delores is my most difficult client—difficult not because of her personality, but because of her needs (my third elephant), for which I had yet to find a solution. I caught myself thinking, *Maybe I can avoid the problem for a day by returning the call at lunchtime.*

As I walked down the hall, I noticed that my elephants were not the only ones on the premises. First came Carlos's elephants. I heard through the grapevine that Carlos was going to quit unless he received a substantial—and well-deserved—raise. I made a mental note to schedule time with him. For whatever reason, Carlos was not making the first move. I did not want to lose such a valuable employee, so I planned to say *hello* to Carlos's elephant myself.

And then there was Andrew, a new client sitting in the waiting area next to his elephant. Andrew had not created a succession plan for his business because he did not know how to tell his son that he planned to leave control to his niece.

And what about Delores Hickey, my most difficult client? For years, Delores and her family had been spending at a deficit. Thanks to large year-end bonuses and lucky investments, Delores always managed to make ends meet in the eleventh hour. The situation was more desperate this year because her business had taken a turn for the worse and her investments were lagging. The banks were breathing down her neck, and although Delores was bringing in $1,200,000 a year, her family was spending $1,500,000 annually. I kept advising Delores to rein in the spending, but Delores did not want to put her family on an allowance. Though she shared her concerns with her husband and children, they considered the conversations business as usual. Delores's mountain of debt was growing, and her panic attacks were increasing in frequency. The solution sounded simple: address the overspending and create a budget. But Delores refused to limit her family members' spending for reasons I did not completely understand.

One thing was certain: by ignoring these elephants, Carlos, Andrew, Delores, and I guaranteed that the problems were not going to resolve themselves positively in most cases. In some way, they **would** take care of themselves, but the outcome would likely not be favorable. I knew that if we did not confront our elephants proactively, the outcomes would cause more discomfort and might lead to disaster.

We all have elephants—those obvious needs, obstacles, or truths that we are somehow ignoring, despite the fact that they desperately need to be addressed for us to feel fulfilled and peaceful. Sometimes these elephants are personal—relationships that are not working, children who have substance abuse problems, financial woes that need to be tamed, or dreams that have not been realized. Often, we have professional elephants in the form of partnerships gone astray, succession planning that needs to be initiated, or goal planning that should be moved to the front of the line.

Say Hello to the Elephants provides business owners, families, and entrepreneurs with a new way to think about their issues, as well as critical tools for addressing problems, reaching clarity about goals, and making effective decisions. We do this through Quadrant Thinking, a process based on Scott Fithian's Planning Horizon™ concept.[1] Quadrant Thinking organizes the problem-solution model into a straightforward, organized progression that first identifies core values and vision, next outlines how to reach the desired goal, and then ensures that the plan is implemented and evaluated. By using Quadrant Thinking, you can say *hello* to your elephants, rope them, and wrangle them out of the room. The good health my business has enjoyed demonstrates the power of Quadrant Thinking: it helps address critical issues so that giant elephants morph into tiny mice.[2]

As its name implies, Quadrant Thinking is a four-part process, and the four sections of *Say Hello to the Elephants* are dedicated to exploring each of these processes in detail. This life-changing information is distilled from both my own experiences and the countless resources dedicated to transformation. In particular, the Quadrant Thinking Conductor at the back of the book will escort you and your advisors through the process by asking specific questions and providing exercises that promote clarity, solutions, implementation, and sustainability.

---

[1] Scott C. Fithian (d. 2006) was an advocate of values-based planning. He considered human capital as important (if not more important) than monetary capital. Fithian authored *Values-Based Estate Planning*, a must-read for anyone serious about creating a legacy and a life of significance.

[2] Or bunnies, if you are the type to jump on a chair at the sight of a mouse.

In **Quadrant One: Clarity**, we examine your motives, consider your values, and create a vision that addresses the situation, leading you to visualize a clear and ideal result. By reaching clarity, you will know the answer to this question: *What will this problem look like when it has been perfectly addressed and eliminated?*

Clarity is the single most important part of the process. Without clarity, "the best-laid plans of mice and men[3] go oft awry," regardless of how crafty our solution, how solid our implementation, or how devout our sustainability plan. Because clarity is the most critical component, this section represents the largest portion of the book.

Quadrant Two: Solutions looks at the steps necessary to reach your ideal life and clarified vision. Here, we examine available solutions and choose the one that is most efficient and effective. The key in this quadrant is to work with the right person (or team) to find solutions that bring you closer to your ideal result. We will discuss the concept of "the trusted advisor" and teach you how to choose an effective team to address needs such as tax planning, succession planning, legacy planning, or life planning.

Quadrant Three: Implementation provides motivation for implementing your solution, as well as an introduction to the idea that confidence is a critical component of clarity planning. When plans go astray, the person responsible for pulling the trigger most likely lacked confidence in his vision or solution. In other words, he did not have clarity.

Quadrant Four: Sustainability explains how to preserve a plan, change a plan, or address new needs over time—making sure that clarity is retained, solutions remain effective, and implementation continues.

---

3 And women!

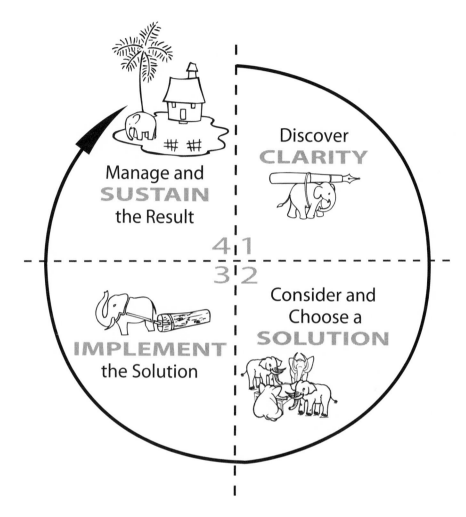

Say Hello to the Elephants is not a self-help book. View it instead as a series of appointments whereby you can leverage my thirty years' experience to create an educating and empowering system.

Imagine that you and I are sitting in my office. During this first session, I will introduce my process to you. We will follow up with a series of sessions, all designed to help you take control of your business, wealth, and ultimately, your life. You might think our conversations will be confined to tax and accountancy issues, but you will be pleasantly surprised. We will look at promising (but challenging) issues in **all** areas of your life. We will find solutions, implement action, and then sustain momentum. The result will be clarity, progress, and confidence. Most importantly, you will be in control of the process.

Too often, new clients who walk into our accountancy, tax, and legacy planning office are overwhelmed with decisions about their business, career, or lives. Because of the intricacies and complications surrounding these issues, clients are accustomed to turning over their financial lives to so-called experts. This is shocking. Who could be more of an expert about **your** life than you? By giving control to an expert, your size-ten feet will likely be crammed into size-eight shoes. Imagine a solution fashioned from whole cloth and finished in the course of a one-hour meeting. Solve your lifetime issues? Not a chance! But if you achieve clarity about your goals, you can guide your advisors to craft personalized and effective strategies that **will** work because they are designed specifically for you.

This applies to all aspects of your life, not just tax planning. From the simple problem to the multi-faceted need, Quadrant Thinking helps you achieve clarity, which means you will be better equipped to design solutions and develop confidence to implement strategies that fit your feet precisely.

Though *Say Hello to the Elephants* is often light in tone, it is heavy in import and thought. After all, clarity is the single most critical component of a successful business venture, a successful partnership, or a successful life.

I have been a certified public accountant for over thirty years. For most of these years, I have been an excellent CPA. I am successful, and my clients appreciate the services my firm provides. Our clients like us, they refer business to us, and they trust us. But from time to time over the first twenty years, our clients simply did not implement the legacy, succession, or exit plans we and their other advisors created for them. When I asked our clients why they had not implemented the plans, their responses were vague. They confirmed that they were happy with our services; they said we were doing a terrific job. Our approaches were solid, thorough, and effective.

But still, certain things simply were not being implemented. I was at a loss until Mitch triggered a revelation.

Mitch was one of my wealthiest clients, and he had been working with us to develop an estate plan. Mitch was a relatively new client, and when we brought him on board, we also met his lawyer, who was considered one of the state's best estate planning attorneys. Between attorney fees and legacy planning fees, Mitch had already spent $2,000,000 on an elaborate and sophisticated estate plan. But despite the fact that his attorney had been pressuring him to implement a plan for twenty-five years, Mitch never signed the document, leaving it ineffective year after year! Mitch's attorney updated the plan annually, and each year Mitch promised—and failed—to sign the plan.

Then Mitch ended his twenty-five-year relationship with his attorney and hired a sole practitioner. It was a strange choice: a multi-millionaire left a huge law firm with vast resources dedicated to the ultra-wealthy in favor of a sole practitioner with great expertise but more limited resources.

However, within nine months of making this shift, Mitch signed his estate plan, implementing a course of action that would eventually transfer $70,000,000 to his children, avoid probate, drastically reduce estate taxes, and chart a course for his family over generations to come.

So what happened to prompt his action?

The sole practitioner, a young attorney named Judy, spent enough time with Mitch to determine why he had not signed his estate planning documents. While Mitch's old attorney thought that Mitch's failure to sign the documents **was** the problem, Judy recognized this as a symptom of a larger problem. Judy learned that Mitch was concerned about the effects of transferring wealth to his children and grandchildren, fearing that his descendants would misuse the money or, worse yet, allow a large inheritance to taint their work ethic. Prior to Judy's intervention, Mitch's lawyer had not spent enough time with Mitch to uncover this concern. Instead, he spent this time offering solutions to save taxes when he should have been gaining insight about his client's concerns. The effect that Mitch's estate plan would have on his family was Mitch's elephant in the room. He wanted his children and grandchildren to meet certain conditions prior to receiving the inheritance, and he felt uncomfortable discussing this with his previous attorney, whose primary concern was transferring wealth, not transferring values.

But once the elephant was identified, the solution became apparent. The trusts he created for his family demanded that certain criteria be met prior to allocation of trust monies. His trust required that his descendants have an advanced education or learn a trade before trust monies would be available, and the more money they earned on their own, the more access they had to trust funds. If Mitch's children participated in philanthropic work, they were rewarded in ways that non-charitable children and grandchildren would not be. In this way, Mitch was able to make sure his money was used to support his values, even after his death. With this assurance in hand, Mitch felt confident signing and implementing his trust documents.

This was when I became an advocate of clarity planning. Because Mitch lacked clarity, the solution Mitch's previous attorney advocated did not resonate with Mitch. It failed to address his elephants. And lacking confidence in his solution, Mitch was unwilling to implement the plan, much less maintain it.

This is why I so strongly emphasize saying *hello* to your elephants. This means not only uncovering and tackling the obvious problems in your business or life, but also acknowledging and addressing your unfulfilled dreams.

One way or another, it all begins by reaching clarity.

CLARITY

Quadrant One | CLARITY

AN OLD MAN IS VISITED BY A GENIE who grants him one wish. The old man can ask for anything he pleases: untold riches, eternal youth, a beautiful home in the country.

After a long, thoughtful pause, the old man says quietly, "I want to live in a world without war."

The genie nods her head. "Your wish is my command," she says. "You will wake up tomorrow in a world without war."

When the old man awakens the next morning, he discovers that the genie has kept her word. The old man now lives in a world without war—for all the other people have disappeared.

This fable captures a profound truth: without clarity, the noblest intentions can lead to unexpected and unfortunate results. This is why clarity is the first and most important quadrant. In this quadrant, you will identify the overarching vision from which you will define your action plan (Quadrant Two: Solutions).

Whether planning your day or planning your life, the first step is to identify in clear, precise terms what your purpose is. The Clarity Quadrant addresses not only a life vision, but also helps to define a simple or complex problem. If you are having a professional conflict, it answers this question: *What would the ideal outcome look like?* The question remains the same when considering a life plan: *What would my ideal life look like?*

| CRITICAL QUESTION |

In any problem, large or small, clarity planning answers one critical question: What does the ideal outcome look like?

In day-to-day life, we are bombarded with choices and options. The choices might be simple: *Should I fire that employee? Should I keep working or make time to exercise?* Or, the choices might be more complex, considering not only today, but also the future: *Should I invest in this company? Where do I want to be in fifteen years? Who will run my business if I cannot or do not want to continue?*

Only by having clarity can we navigate through these choices. While making these choices, we always need to understand *why*. Why are we doing this? That answer enables us to chart our course and avoid life's inevitable distractions.

Having defined goals and an established vision also gives us a standard that helps us to choose among alternatives. If a client wants to plan his estate, how much of his estate should he allocate to charity? Without clear goals, that question is impossible to answer. If his aim is to use a portion of his wealth to serve broad societal purposes, he will be largely dissatisfied if his estate plan assumes that his goal is to ensure his heirs receive as much wealth as possible. On the other hand, if a person's goal is to equally divide his assets among his children, regardless of the tax consequences, he will not be satisfied with a plan that allocates resources to a charity to avoid taxes. Either choice might be a good one, so long as it fulfills a person's clearly stated vision.

Trying to function without defined goals is like trying to pilot a plane without a destination. You will still end up somewhere, but the destination will not be of your choosing—and the landing will probably be bumpy. The same is true in any endeavor. A person who does not develop an estate plan will still have his wealth go somewhere, but a large portion will be sucked up by estate taxes, and the assets will likely go through the costly, drawn-out process of probate—probably not the outcome he would have chosen had he defined his goals and then implemented an appropriate solution. Likewise, a business owner without a clear vision can only move toward a fuzzy and uncertain future.

Defining our goals puts us in control of our lives, and enables us to **feel** in control of our lives. Without goals, we still have to make decisions, but they will be short range and reactive. That is not a path to success.

To achieve clarity is to stop being a rat in a maze and to become like a speeding jet, whipping by the distractions and focused on the end goal. And though success cannot ever be assured, a plane is much more likely to arrive at its destination if it has charted its course.

SETTING CLEAR GOALS

Most of us have a general sense of why we engage in specific activities, but clarity extends beyond generalities to encompass three characteristics:

1. Specific
2. Measurable
3. Anchored to values

For example, if your plan is to grow your business, saying, "I want to build my bottom line" is not enough. Instead, a clear goal would state, "I want to increase my company's net profits by 15 percent next fiscal year so that I can send my children to the best possible schools and honor my commitment to education."

Specific ← I want to increase my company's net profits

Measurable ← by 15 percent next fiscal year

Anchored to Values ← so that I can send my children to the best possible schools and honor my commitment to education.

The value of goal setting is so widely recognized that it has almost become a bromide. Countless books philosophize *ad nauseam* about leading the examined life, setting goals, and realizing potential. The focus on goal setting is so high that it is in danger of becoming trivialized. And yet despite all of this, most people do not have clearly defined goals. They do not have clarity of vision.

With such an influx of business coaches, books that promise transformation, and life planning workshops in today's society, how can this be? How can there be such a lack of clarity in a culture so focused on and fascinated with clarity? We will discuss this paradox throughout this section, starting with the roadblocks to clarity.

ROADBLOCKS TO CLARITY

Roadblock #1: Clarity takes effort. Contrary to the hedonist fantasy that indulging in our whims and fleeting desires will lead us to happiness, knowing what we want is not easy. Even the desire to make more money is not self-evidently in our interest. We would all **like** more money, but clarity means asking the question: *Is there some other goal I am after that takes precedence over increasing my wealth?*

To set goals requires that you know yourself—and that takes work. Many times, we do things because we think we *have* to do them. But in setting goals, you acknowledge that you don't *have* to do anything: you only have to do something if you want to contribute to a goal that you willfully select. You don't have to go to work. You don't have to go into business. You don't have to keep the same employees just because they show up for work. You don't have to contribute to your alma mater simply because the development officer bought you lunch. You don't have to live where you live. You don't have to pay your bills. You don't have to exercise.

You don't have to do any of this…

…unless you want certain outcomes. Clarity is about putting forth the effort to make sure that the outcomes you receive are predictable and intentional. The result of those intentional outcomes will promote a fulfilling life. We call this "intentional planning."

Roadblock #2: Clarity forces us to decide between competing ends. We all have many things we would like to do. I want to make more money, learn a new hobby, read more, exercise regularly, travel, and spend more time with my family—but the clock resets after twenty-four hours. Clarity often means having to make difficult tradeoffs. It's not easy for most people to consciously decide to spend less time with their families so they can make their businesses more successful. But too often when they fail to make decisions consciously, they end up doing so reactively.

Instead of telling their family that they will have to spend less time together, and then religiously guarding that allotted time, they end up disappointing their family by unexpectedly missing dinners and canceling plans.

To be sure, even when tradeoffs are made consciously, they can be difficult. But when tradeoffs are made unconsciously and haphazardly, the results generally lead to disaster, unhappiness, and regret. Moments are lost, relationships injured, and opportunities squandered.

Roadblock #3: Clarity forces us to face difficult facts.
Clarity sometimes forces us to confront truths we would rather ignore. If I am planning my estate, I might have to acknowledge the painful fact that one of my children[1] is not responsible enough to handle a large inheritance. Or, if I set clearly defined performance standards for my employees, I might have to accept that an employee I like as a person will need to be fired. But evading an unpleasant fact does not make it disappear; instead, ignoring an elephant turns a small health ailment into an untreatable disease.

Roadblock #4: Clarity forces us to take responsibility.
To set a goal is to commit to taking the action necessary to achieve it. When a person says, "This is my goal," he is implicitly saying, "I am taking responsibility for achieving this goal." To set a goal is to put excuses aside and acknowledge that **you** exert the most control over your success or failure. This is a reality some of us would rather avoid.

Without clarity planning, you might not ever find solutions to the problems that are plaguing you. You might go through life wondering why things never go the way you like, running your business into the ground, and dealing with maladjusted family members by ignoring their problems.

But by setting a vision and creating clear goals, you enable yourself to have greater control of the outcomes. When considered a tool to intentionally take a person from Point A to Point B, the roadblocks become benefits.

---

[1] Note to my children: there is no subtle meaning in this statement.

Benefit #1: Clarity takes effort. This effort is exactly why the accomplishments are so sweet. Without the energy exerted to reach a goal, its accomplishment would be meaningless.

Benefit #2: Clarity allows us to decide between competing ends. Clarity allows us to prioritize, delegate, or eliminate those things that are unimportant and replace them with things that truly are important.

Benefit #3: Clarity allows us to face difficult facts. By obtaining clarity, we come to terms with reality. This increased fund of knowledge makes us more likely to create effective strategies and reach our goals.

Benefit #4: Clarity allows us to take responsibility. By designing intentional strategies pointed toward a specific goal, you can claim your success as your own. Let luck, destiny, and chance try to steal your thunder! They will all be unsuccessful—the fruits of your labor are yours to enjoy.

Turn roadblocks into benefits by seeing the opportunity in every obstacle:

Roadblock 1: Clarity takes effort.	**Benefit 1:** Clarity takes effort.
Roadblock 2: Clarity forces us to decide between competing ends.	**Benefit 2:** Clarity allows us to decide between competing ends.
Roadblock 3: Clarity forces us to face difficult facts.	**Benefit 3:** Clarity allows us to face difficult facts.
Roadblock 4: Clarity forces us to take responsibility.	**Benefit 4:** Clarity allows us to take responsibility.

When considering the roadblocks and upsides of clarity planning, let's start with the most obvious: Clarity planning takes effort.

CLARITY PLANNING TAKES EFFORT, AND PAIN IS SWELL.

IMAGINE YOU TELL YOUR FITNESS TRAINER, Doyle, that you have always wanted to run a marathon.

"No problem," he says (of the 26.2-mile race). "It will be easy."

You smile at him and say, "Swell."

So you are off and running, expecting it to be a piece of cake based on what your fitness trainer has told you. It will be calming, he says. You will probably have one epiphany after another, similar to those deep, transformational moments during yoga. Doyle leads you to believe that running the marathon will be kind of like relaxing in a Jacuzzi, but different.

You set off running on your first training session. You start hopeful and full of confidence.

Then reality sets in. Your heart is about to burst out of your chest, and you are panting like a thirsty dog. You are convinced that your toenails will rub off, your arches will fall, and you will have shin splints, sweat rashes, strained Achilles tendons, blisters, chafing, and various knee and back ailments along the way.[2] You have only run a half-mile before you decide that running is quite awful.

Swell? More like swelling!

I am simply not cut out for this, you decide, reflecting on Doyle's claim that it should be easy.

On Day One of training, you quit.

---

2 You might be a hypochondriac.

This is the problem with most clarity-planning processes. Although it might seem that clarity should be intuitive, the process of reaching clarity is not always easy. Clarity can be difficult to achieve. It does not have to be painful, but it often is. Our choices muddy the waters. Our responsibilities add pressure, and our setbacks seem impossible to overcome.

Why are we talking about pain so early in a book that is intended to be motivational? The process of attaining clarity can be painful, and if your advisors hype clarity planning as an easy, effortless task, you might quit the minute you experience pain. And to be sure, pain can be an integral part of clarity planning, which has three essential corollaries:

1. You must accept pain as part of the process. It comes with the territory. If it were easy (as Doyle and countless advisors and books might have you believe), everyone would have clarity. Stop and think for a moment: how many folks do you know that have clarity?

2. To reach clarity, you must commit to endure the pain. "What matters most is how well you walk through the fire," author Charles Bukowski said. Being aware of the process means fewer surprises.

3. You must be patient. No one has ever trained for and completed a 26.2-mile race during a thirty-minute lunch break![3] Patience means that you push through the pain, knowing it will subside, and when you reach your goal, the pain will have been well worth it.

Because mental tenacity is such a critical part of reaching your goal, we spend most of our time in the Clarity Quadrant. By their very nature, elephants are mammoth.[4] Acknowledging them can be challenging, unpleasant,

---

[3] But Joey Chestnut, who holds the world record in competitive hot dog eating contests, once ate sixty-six hot dogs, plus buns, in twelve minutes.

[4] The largest elephant weighed more than twenty-six thousand pounds and was nearly fourteen feet tall. Mammoths, on the other hand, usually grew only to about seven feet and seven thousand pounds. So while elephants **are** mammoth, mammoths are not quite as mammoth.

and even painful—at least initially. When facing them, you must be able to answer *yes* to the following question: *Do I really want to be doing this?*

In your darkest hour, when the forces of the universe seem to be working against you, if the goal you have set for yourself is something you genuinely want to accomplish—if you have achieved clarity—then the answer will always be *yes*.

The desire to achieve your goal drives the will you have to pursue that goal. It drives the belief you have in yourself. No matter how intense the discomfort, the mind must surrender before the body will. While running a marathon, a runner often hits the proverbial "wall." His mind starts screaming: *Stop! Stop! I cannot take this anymore!*

The truth of the matter is: he can. He has got to take a few more steps, and then a few more, and then a few more. If he really, truly, bottom-of-his-heart, core-of-his-soul wants it—if he has clarity—he can keep going, despite the pain or, perhaps, **because** of the pain.

Pain, at least when it has passed, can be palliative. Imagine for a moment a world in which we could set ambitious, challenging goals and then turn around and attain them without sacrificing a single ounce of blood, sweat, or tears. Not only would that take the "accomplish" out of the accomplishment, but it would also turn your ambitious goals into monotony. You probably would not want to achieve those goals any more. At best, the accomplishments would lack significant meaning.

Maybe your trainer, Doyle, disagrees. "Goals that are easy to reach would not be boring or monotonous," he says. "That would be fantastic. We could have our cake and eat it too! Sign me up—I love German chocolate cake!"

You should fire Doyle.

Pain gives meaning to our desire and ability to reach goals. It strengthens us, builds our self-confidence and self-worth, and gives us the experience we need to get through the next round of pain. When you have fought for years and years to reach the top—and in the course of those years you have been beaten down, failed on numerous occasions, and rejected by more people than you can count—you will know, beyond a shadow of a doubt, that you have earned it once you get to the top. The pain you endured will make the reward sweeter. The scrapes and scars are all badges of courage proving you were challenged. The mettle was tested, and the mettle won.

The pain is priceless.

You hire a new trainer, Lance. Lance's favorite movie is *Predator*[5] about a U.S. Special Forces unit under attack by a hideous creature from outer space known as "the Predator." Lance's favorite moment is when a fellow soldier informs the tobacco-chewing Blain that Blain is bleeding. Blain keeps chewing his tobacco, scoping out the terrain, matter-of-factly stating, "I ain't got time to bleed."

And neither do you. When you have clarity, much of the pain is incidental. The reward makes the pain irrelevant.

Take Theodore Geisel. In college, Theodore was voted the least likely to succeed.[6] Though his art and writing professors disagreed, Theodore felt he had a knack for drawing and writing, so he sent his work to a number of publishing companies, all of whom rejected his books like clockwork. Twenty-seven publishers said *no*.[7] And then, publisher twenty-eight said *yes*. With that, Theodore Seuss Geisel became Dr. Seuss.

Certainly, being rejected or meeting obstacles can be painful. Disappointment, frustration, and anxiety are normal. But whether that pain blocks you from moving forward is up to you. You can take rejection and let it cut deep, let the pain seer into your being. Or you can say, "I am only looking for one publisher to say *yes*. This is not the one, but I ain't got time to bleed, so I will just keep looking," and move on.

There's no getting around it: some things are going to hurt. Confronting partnership problems is not easy, nor is it easy to plan for succession, take a new risk, or end a relationship. There is no shortcut. You must have clarity and people like Lance ministering your strength within.

Speaking of Lance, you tell him about your goal of running a marathon. He nods his head. With understanding and support, he says, "Your goal is worthy, and you can do it. It is going to take some time. Many people will not believe that you will succeed. You will have a lot of close calls—a lot of times

---

[5] Lance is right. This movie **is** pretty great, not just because of the incredible action sequences, but because it stars two—count 'em, two!—United States governors: Arnold of California and Jesse "The Body" Ventura of Minnesota.

[6] They don't sell "My child was voted **least** likely to succeed" bumper stickers.

[7] Those Grinches!

when you think you cannot do it. Your body will shake. You will feel discouraged, but if you are sure you want to do it, if you want to call yourself a marathoner—a title only 0.13 percent of the population can claim—you can move past the pain. No matter how many disappointments or setbacks you encounter, you can do it. I will be there to help. You are unstoppable."

You look at Lance and say, "Swell."

Believe in a bigger future.

WE HAVE BRIEFLY DISCUSSED THE IDEA that clarity forces us to face competing ends. Although this might seem like a roadblock, it actually encourages us to recognize that the future holds indefinite opportunities.

A profound and deep sadness sets in when we have no exciting dreams on the horizon. On the other hand, when we have clarity, we have hope. Clarity gives us something to look forward to, something to strive for. Every day of working toward a vision brings us closer to a dream. Even if all we do on a particular day is **think** about what our new business legacy will look like, we know that we are one day closer to achieving that goal.

The power of thought is powerful indeed. So is the power of belief. Believing that things will improve in tandem with the effort you put forward is vital. No matter how dire your situation, believing in yourself gives you a glimpse of the light at the end of the tunnel—and moves you closer to that light. To **have** a bigger future, we need to **believe** in a bigger future. We have to be optimistic and hopeful,[8] and we need to surround ourselves with people, situations, and opportunities that remind us of, mirror, and encourage this hope.

Have you ever noticed that when somebody around you yawns, you also start to yawn? Heck, just because you are reading the word *yawn*, you may start to yawn. This thought-action reflex happens with laughter as well. Even if you do not know why someone is laughing, you will probably get the giggles if you are sitting next to someone who busts into a fit of laughter.

---

8 My buddy Confucius said, "He who has hope, has everything."

Once upon a time, I was attending a tax symposium that reached stupendous levels of boredom. Soon, I began to tune out and think about the movie I had seen the evening before, *A Fish Called Wanda*. Unlike tax symposiums, the movie is hilarious, which is why I began to laugh. Recognizing that my laughter was inappropriate, I tried to stifle it, which only made me laugh louder. At first the people surrounding me looked at me like I was a loon. But then they started to laugh with me. They had no idea that a scene from *A Fish Called Wanda* was running through my mind. They just saw someone laughing, and that was all they needed. Soon my entire section was laughing, and the symposium suddenly became a ton of fun.[9] This thought-action reflex happens with laughter and yawning because it happens with everything.

Everything.

Unfortunately, that includes feelings of negativity. If you are constantly negative or pessimistic, people will not want to be around you because it makes them feel sad and gloomy. Negative energy perpetrates more negative energy, just as positive energy creates more positive energy. This is not a platitude, but a simple truth.

It is important to believe in a bigger future not because we want everyone to be cheerful, but because your future will not be bigger if you do not believe it is going to be bigger. If you believe, then those around you are more likely to believe—which creates the providential conditions you need to gain whatever you are after.

On the other hand, if you believe—out of frustration—that things are going to stay the same, or that they are only going to get worse, you will be right! Expecting failure is not an experiment I recommend trying.

You might have heard of a movie called *The Secret*. Consistent with my novel idea that there are no new ideas, *The Secret* was actually little more than a clever marketing idea that promised ancient wisdom. The "secret" was simple: think positive thoughts and you will have abundance; think negative thoughts and you will suffer a drought.

---

9 Question: What does an accountant use for birth control? Answer: His personality.

The Secret was controversial for a host of reasons. First of all, it was no secret.[10] Countless authors have written about this very topic for years, including Napoleon Hill, who wrote *Think and Grow Rich* way back in 1937. Despite this, some people say *The Secret* changed their lives; others hated every moment of it. Regardless, it did bring an important concept into the mainstream: if you walk with a cloud over your head, rain will fall on you. If you refuse to walk in the shade, you will always find yourself standing in sunshine.

I recommend a simple exercise that illustrates the importance of having something positive to anticipate. Pick an activity you really love. Perhaps you love golfing, or maybe you love making tiny birds out of colored paper. Whatever it is, resist doing it for longer than usual. Instead, set a date in the near future to resume the activity.

In the meantime, pay attention to how much you think about and look forward to that activity. Within a few days, you will notice that the promise of doing something you really enjoy will bring a smile to your face, even during hectic or tiring times. You will be soothed as soon as you think: *It is crazy in the office right now, but that is okay because next week I will be participating in our Civil War re-enactment.*

Having small things to look forward to—a weekend trip, a golf game with your business partners, or a meeting with an important client—is gratifying, and when the stakes are higher, this gratification multiplies.

This is always true, but it is especially important when the chips are down. Finding something to look forward to can be the difference between success and failure.

This is what I mean by "believing in a bigger future." In simple terms, it means that you have something to look forward to, and you have set goals that are motivating. If you are highly accomplished, it means that you have a source of inspiration urging you to keep moving forward, despite past successes. And if you have struggled to reach success, it means that you believe that you can overcome your obstacles.

---

10 And even if it was, it was a lousy secret. When someone tells me a secret, I want an actual secret, a juicy bit of gossip that I have to pinky-swear to take to my grave. Telling someone that the Law of Attraction is a secret is kind of like telling someone gravity is a secret. Boooring.

You might be thinking, *Yep. This is all great. Too bad I'm seventy-five years old. Not much of a future left for me.* Believing in a bigger future is not reserved for the young. In fact, it is particularly important for those reaching retirement. How many times have we heard of someone with a productive career that retires, only to immediately fall ill and die? Some analysts and therapists believe this happens because when the feeling of productivity leaves, so too does the desire to live. Believing in a bigger future means that we believe in another twenty, thirty, or forty years of productive achievement after retirement.

The only way to truly accomplish your goals is to believe that you will. Don't take my word for it. Listen to singer Helen Reddy, who said, "I always believed that I could make it or I would never have spent so many years trying to get here."

For Reddy, "here" was life as a successful singer—no easy task. But she did it because she believed.[11]

Once there were two men, Jeff and Geoff. They lived on opposite sides of the same town. Both owned garden retail businesses, and both had reached high levels of material success.

But this is where the similarities ended.[12] Jeff's glass was always half-full. Geoff's glass was always half-empty. Jeff wanted continued growth—not only in his professional life, but also in his personal life. Geoff believed his current level of success was at a plateau. *This is as good as it gets*, he thought.

Geoff plodded through his days, never truly happy. He was interested in expanding his business, but he did nothing to pursue this dream, assuming it was out of his control. The thought of accomplishing such a feat seemed distant and overwhelming, so he never bothered to try. He hired and fired employees, complained about his "cheap" customers, and was generally gloomy. People did not enjoy being around Geoff. He attracted clients who valued low-cost over relationships, so they did not refer business his way. *Even if I wanted to expand my business, I couldn't*, thought Geoff, who had failed to develop the network or resources to expand his business.

Across town, Jeff was a different story.

---

11 It helped that she is strong. She is invincible.
12 For one thing, Jeff's parents knew how to spell.

Although Jeff was not satisfied with the current state of his business, he saw it as a necessary stepping stone toward his bigger goals. He was enthusiastic about his work, recognizing that each day brought him closer to realizing his goals. He followed Monty Python's sage advice to always look on the bright side of life. Every week Jeff took small steps toward expanding his business, which he eventually wanted to franchise. Because he knew the power of referrals, he made sure to nurture relationships with his clients, who were loyal, despite his higher-than-average prices. Jeff knew he would one day be running a medium-sized garden center, which would eventually go head-to-head with the Lowe's and Home Depots of the world. Jeff devoured business books, attended seminars, and cultivated mentor relationships within his community. He enjoyed doing these things as much as he enjoyed envisioning his future franchise.

On Jeff's worst days in his tiny garden center, this dream of a bigger future helped Jeff maintain his positive attitude. And because of this positive attitude, people liked being around Jeff. His positive attitude attracted positive people, who supported and encouraged Jeff's dream, which in turn helped Jeff stay focused. His employees were loyal, which meant he paid little in turnover costs. His customers loved the friendly feeling of the store. They enjoyed talking to him and hearing about his future plans. They were willing to pay the slightly higher prices in exchange for superior service, so Jeff's business had a healthy bottom line. Because of the upscale feel of his store, and because of his sunny disposition, he met investors, entrepreneurs, and advisors who were interested in seeing him succeed.

When Jeff was ready to implement his plan, he had a large network of helpful colleagues and loyal customers. And this is how Jeff developed his franchise, exactly as he envisioned it.

CLARITY IS THE ENEMY
OF THE STATUS QUO.

MERE OBSERVATION SHOULD BE PROOF enough that dour Geoff is not alone in his poor attitude. Heart disease might kill more Americans than any other disease, but resigning power over your own life kills more American dreams than anything else.

Many of us are not empowered people who own and control the direction of our lives. We speak in generalities about life's possibilities, but most of us think dreams are only dreams.

Even with the best of attitudes, we might fail to get **there**, simply because we do not know where **there** is. The fastest way to fight past an obstacle preventing success—whether it is the glass ceiling, the closed mind of an investor, or a partnership conflict—is by reaching clarity. Reaching clarity about our dreams, wants, and goals, and then defeating the elephants that stand in our way, guarantees movement in a new direction.

This is not a novel concept. If you do not like the status quo, make a change. It sounds simple, but how many of us have held onto jobs, investments, or even partners that we absolutely do not want to keep? We refuse to change, even though change would guarantee that we no longer have the same lousy job, lousy investment, or lousy partner.

"Wait a minute," you might say. "If I change, I might end up with another lousy job, investment, or partner."

Yes, you might. But consider what will happen if you do not change. If you keep a lousy status quo, you are **guaranteed** to have a lousy job, investment, or partner. Hedge your bets and play the odds. If you have clarity of vision, the gamble is not such a big one.

Despite being a twenty-five-year-old man[13], I have always been inspired by the words of the Cheshire Cat. His words spoke to me when I was a teenager, and they speak to me today:

"Would you tell me, please, which way I ought to go from here?" Alice *speaks to the Cheshire Cat.*

"That depends a good deal on where you want to get to," said the Cat.

"I don't care much where—" said Alice.

"Then it doesn't matter which way you go," said the Cat.

The reverse of this is that if you know where you are going, the road becomes very specific. If you live in Atlanta and want to fly to New York, stop going through Butte, Montana.[14]

Admittedly, I am simplifying things, but I will not apologize for it. The issue **is** simple, and it is critical. If you are unhappy with the status quo, you must decide where you want to be. In doing so, the direction becomes clear and the status quo is joyfully endangered. Later, we will discuss the idea that the solution becomes much easier to identify when direction is defined. Likewise, the status quo is defeated when you set out in a new direction.

And if you think you are satisfied with the status quo, be assured that you are living an illusion. Life is an ocean of experience. I have never seen an ocean that does not move. What works for you today might not work tomorrow. What is productive and useful today might not serve you in the future. You might not want to change, but you must or your balance and control will be lost—just like someone standing in the tide is bound to lose his balance if he is rigid and unwilling to shift. Clarity is the landmark you establish in life's ocean that keeps you moving toward your desires.

---

13 Okay, I am actually in my fifties, but I am an accountant. I play with numbers all day.
14 Unless you also want to: 1) visit a giant copper mine; or 2) attend Evel Knievel Days.

F O C U S   O N   T H E   G O A L ,
N O T   T H E   D I S T R A C T I O N S .

IMAGINE THAT YOU ARE WATCHING a boring movie. Let's pick *The English Patient*.[15] While watching the film, you become more and more bored, but you notice a palm tree in the background that looks a lot like your Aunt Edna's head. Now you are fixated on the palm tree, which causes Ralph Fiennes[16] and everything else on the screen to become a blurry background. The palm tree, much more interesting than the movie, becomes your center of focus. Your goal becomes this: focus on the palm tree so as to not be distracted by the lame movie.

You are fondly reminiscing about the time your Aunt Edna accidentally served cat food as an appetizer when the camera angle changes and you lose sight of the palm tree. You are distracted by Ralph and the "plot." In the blink of an eye, your interest transitions to boredom. You find yourself listlessly counting the seconds until the movie ends, willing time to move forward.

The way we look at things, and what we choose to focus on, shapes our point of view. If you focus on the palm tree and your Aunt Edna's head, you will find *The English Patient* a delight. If you focus on the distractions (Ralph Fiennes and the "plot"), the movie is painfully boring.

In short, clarity requires that you fixate not on the distractions, but on the goal.

---

15 Among the worst movies ever made, *The English Patient* went on to receive nine Academy Awards. It's a wild, wild world.
16 A name Ralph claims is pronounced "Reyf Fahyns."

And what are some distractions that can keep us from focusing on the goal? Distractions can come in the form of people, setbacks, fear of failure, or even fear of success.

ILLEGITIMI NON CARBORUNDUM[17]

Though I sincerely hope everyone I know is supporting my efforts and cheering me on, the truth of the matter is that some people (consciously or subconsciously) are trying to hold me back. It is of no personal benefit to my most important client that I land a bigger account. Indeed, their fear that I might get too busy to pay attention to their needs prevents some clients from referring their friends to me. And no matter how evolved my business partners are, I know they want to outperform me.

Let me be clear: competition is healthy, as is the desire to hold on to those people and situations that most benefit you. But your friends, colleagues, and clients can quickly become your enemies if your ability to move forward threatens their own sense of security. Whether a case of greed, insecurity, or old-fashioned jealously, people may not want to see you reach the next plateau, especially if they remain firmly seated on their status quos. So they sit in their cubicles, occasionally popping their heads out like nervous prairie dogs to say, "FYI, you cannot do it." And then they go back into their burrows, hoping you will join them.[18]

These people do not necessarily intend to resist your success; some are simply afraid of change. Your change might force them to change, and because they have not read this book, they are scared, scared, scared! Whatever the case, your job is to identify the people holding you back, and then consciously decide to ignore them.

This does not mean that you forever isolate yourself from your best friend or a partner who fails to support you. It means recognizing that people invested in the status quo might see change as the tidal wave that puts them out of balance. Their advice might be harmful instead of helpful. Your job is to first understand the back-story that accompanies a person's advice. When someone provides useful information offered from a place of authenticity,

---

17 Not Latin for "don't let the bastards grind you down."
18 Be sure to check out the prairie dog exhibit at the Los Angeles zoo, and eat a hot dog, while you are at it.

you might want to take the advice. But if a naysayer uncomfortable with the progress you are making starts offering harmful, crushing, or deflating advice, disregard it, and focus on the goal. If your failure justifies a person's inertia, ignore his advice.

Fortunately for him, Paul Potts found the strength to ignore all those who did not believe in him. Perhaps you have heard of Paul Potts, a young man from Wales who barely scratched out a living selling cell phones. His childhood dream was to sing opera. Not surprisingly, he was often bullied in school. Had he focused on the distractions, he would probably still be selling mobile phones.

But one day, Paul seized the opportunity to audition for the popular British television show, *Britain's Got Talent*. His clarity of vision allowed him to see the opportunity for what it was. When we know specifically what we are seeking, we can grab opportunities that present themselves and move toward our ideal situation. As Paul nervously told the three judges that he planned to sing opera, he could have been distracted by the judges' obvious doubt.

Then he started singing "Nessum Dorma," a song the judges and the audience had probably never heard. His skills were so impressive that he brought the crowd members to their feet. Many were in tears, including one of the judges. Paul Potts ignored the bullies at school, his co-workers who thought his dreams of singing opera were mere fantasy, and the judges who were skeptical of his abilities.

They were all on the sidelines as Potts focused on his goal.

Today, Paul Potts is an opera star.

SETBACKS ARE A TERRIBLE THING TO WASTE

Going into tax season a few years back, I lost my executive assistant, whom I hired despite the fact that all indicators advised against the hire. The truth is that I hired her because I liked her, disregarding everything I previously learned to be true. I knew from using the Kolbe System[19] that she had a low probability of success in that position. And when she and I realized that she

---

[19] The Kolbe System is a system that gauges the proper instinctive fit for a position.

was not right for the position, she quit. On February 18, two short months before the dreaded April 15 filing deadline, I was suddenly in a pretty dire situation. A giant setback? I would say so!

I could have called my assistant a creep and complained about the mess she created. Instead, I analyzed the situation and considered why I had gotten into this position.

Then I learned from it. I offered myself the same tolerance toward mistakes that I offer my employees. I reminded myself that setbacks are a terrible thing to waste, and I recommitted to the Kolbe System. A person should not dwell on a mistake so long as he learns from it. In this way, a setback can become an important learning tool.

If we lose clarity, or if we never reach clarity, a temporary setback can cause more damage than necessary. Unfortunately, upon failing to meet a smaller goal, most people's natural inclination is to assume a major goal is unreachable. But Byung-Hyun Kim can tell you that this is simply untrue.

In 2001, the Arizona Diamondbacks faced the mighty New York Yankees in the World Series. In Game Five, the Diamondbacks were ahead in the ninth inning when Diamondback relief pitcher, Byung-Hyun Kim, gave up a home run, and the Yankees won the game.

The next night, Byung-Hyun Kim gave the Yankees another home run pitch. Kim's spirit was crushed. He collapsed into the fetal position on the mound. Kim was distracted by a setback, by one loss.

And to be sure, it **was** nothing more than one loss. In fact, it was nothing more than one rotten pitch, and the pitch did not define Byung-Hyun Kim or the World Series.

Yet Kim assumed the fetal position, totally defeated on the mound. The Diamondback's catcher, on the other hand, knew that one loss—even though it was the Diamondback's second loss in a row with only one game left—did not mean the loss of the entire series.

While Kim was defining his life by one setback, the catcher had clarity and could not be distracted. Because of his clarity of vision—his desire to keep pushing toward the World Series title—he was not discouraged, not even for a moment. Without hesitation, catcher Rod Barajas rushed to the mound and confidently consoled Byung-Hyun Kim.

And as any Yankee or Diamondback fan can tell you, the Diamondbacks went on to win the next game, and the 2001 World Series.

FAILURE IS IN THE EYE OF THE BEHOLDER

Thomas Edison said, "If I find 10,000 ways something won't work, I haven't failed. I am not discouraged, because every wrong attempt discarded is another step forward." If Thomas Edison did not have that kind of clarity, you might be reading this book by candlelight.[20]

Michael Jordan missed more than nine thousand shots and lost over three hundred games in his career. Like Byung-Hyun Kim, he was entrusted with the sole responsibility of winning or losing a game—and at least twenty-five times, he missed game-winning baskets. As Jordan says, "I have failed over and over and over again in my life. And that is precisely why I succeed."

Steve Jobs, founder and CEO of Apple Computers, dropped out of college and was later disempowered by the board of directors of the very company he founded. In 2007, he was listed as *Fortune Magazine's* most powerful businessman.

Abe Lincoln was almost forced into bankruptcy. In fact, the list of those who have declared bankruptcy reads like a *Who's Who* in American history, and it includes Walt Disney, Mark Twain, Oscar Wilde, and countless other businessmen and celebrities.

The point is that everyone has failed, been disappointed, and been afraid to do something. The difference is that those who are committed to a vision—those who have clarity—do not accept a sense of defeat as an appropriate response, at least not for long.

THE NEVER-ENDING HORIZON OF SUCCESS

Having the clarity to anticipate the outcomes of successful goals allows us to welcome new circumstances and responsibilities rather than fear them.

When I began my career many years ago, my goal was to earn more than the maximum Social Security wage, which was $8,000 at the time. The first year, I made $8,000, but then the minimum was raised to $10,000; the year after, I made $10,000, while the minimum again increased to $12,000.

I was living in something Dan Sullivan of the Strategic Coach® Inc. calls "the Gap," and I felt like a failure. The Gap occurs when a person measures himself by how far he has to go instead of by how far he has already traveled.

---

20 High-five, Tom!

I had increased my income by a whopping 50 percent in just two years, yet I felt inadequate. My measure of success created a baseline whereby I was looking at where I **wasn't** instead of how far I had come.

Imagine a hiker who sets off to conquer a mountain. He stands at the base of the mountain, thinking, *That doesn't look so far.* As he starts climbing, he gains more and more perspective. *Surely I must be almost there,* he thinks, but the mountaintop stills appears a distant dream. The climber has two choices. He can turn around, gauge the distance he has already traveled, smile, and keep trucking up the hill, or he can keep scratching his head as to why he has not reached that elusive mountaintop, plop down and eat his sandwich before heading back down the hill.

Dan Sullivan provides the image of a sailor on the ocean, always trying to reach the horizon. You may never reach that horizon, and this scares some people.

Any movement toward success changes the status quo and raises the bar. We use terms like rocketing to success, reaching for the stars, and shooting for the moon. We don't say, "Boy, I'm really traveling to a new county by pursuing this business endeavor!"

Progressing to new heights and breaking through is uncomfortable. The fear that accompanies these changes can be as paralyzing as the fear of failure. By working through a process of discovery, you can anticipate these changes and ask yourself if they reflect what you want. If they do, you are free to focus on the overarching goal, which will integrate these changes so that they become a welcome part of your life.

YOU CANNOT IGNORE YOUR WAY TO SUCCESS

One of my dear friends is a successful partner at his law firm. He is among the top 5 percent of U.S. wealth holders, yet year after year, we have the same conversation over a glass of scotch.

"I cannot believe how much I have to pay in taxes," he tells me.

Although he knows he should make quarterly payments, he overspends each year and has too little money to cover his tax bill.

Because of my friend's woeful spending habits, he refused to hire me for years, telling me the same thing when I offered my help.

"I would be ashamed to have you look at my finances," he said.

Instead, my friend hired an accountant he did not know, who filed an extension each year on my friend's behalf. Before each October deadline, my friend would scramble to file and pay his taxes. His modus operandi was to apply for a loan to cover his tax bill.

On top of the interest on the bank loan, my friend also paid penalties and interest to the IRS and state. Had he paid his taxes on time in April, he would have saved the penalties and interest—and on a $150,000 tax bill, we aren't talking chump change.

Imagine now that you are in my friend's shoes, and the IRS comes knocking at your door.

"Howdy there," the IRS says. "You owe me $155,000."

You slam the door, close the curtains, and duck behind your couch.

The next day, the phone rings. "Howdy there," says the IRS. "You owe me $160,000." You quickly hang up.

A week later, you receive a note in the mail. "Howdy there," writes the IRS. "You owe me $175,000." You file the letter in your "to do" folder, which sits under a pile of books on your desk.

When you receive the next letter (this time saying you owe $190,000), you think: *I really should do something about this*—before sticking the letter in a file. Out of sight, out of mind.

The next month, you receive another letter. "Howdy, jackass," writes the IRS. "You owe us more than $200,000. We have placed a lien on your property and notified all of your clients that your wages are being garnished."

You are shocked into action. Suddenly, you rush to the bank, move money around, and find a way to pay the now $200,000 tax bill—which amounts to an extra $50,000 in penalties and interest,[21] simply because you chose to ignore the problem.

When confronted with a problem, whether financial, spiritual, or personal, you can rest assured that the problem will resolve itself whether you take action or not. The question is: **will** the resolution be the one you would have chosen? If you do not have the clarity of purpose that drives your actions, the resolution most likely **will not** be the one you would have chosen.

So how do you find your elephants? Let's go hunting.

---

21 Am I exaggerating? Not by much!

FINDING YOUR ELEPHANTS
AND PROCRASTINATION.

TAX SEASON IS FAST-PACED. We have looming deadlines, the printer jams, the router fails, or an employee spreads a virus (physical or electronic) to the entire office. Though I always have plenty of time for my clients, I do not always spend as much time as I should on my business's needs or on myself.

Several years ago, when I discovered Quadrant Thinking, I had an epiphany: I am often tempted to use my preoccupation with clients as an excuse to ignore the elephants in the room.

Some elephants do not need to be found. They are large, obvious, and right in front of our face. But from time to time, some of us simply want to push them aside and deal with them later.

Before noticing the frequency at which I ignored my elephants because of client issues, I would have handled a human relations problem as follows.

At half past five in the evening, I am running late and will not make it on time to the six o'clock dinner I scheduled with my daughter. I have a mountain of paperwork to finish before leaving for a three-day business trip. My partner enters my office to tell me about a problem with one of my employees.

Short-tempered and feeling strained, I simply say, "I do not have time for this. I will deal with it when I return."

I return to my paperwork, and at six o'clock, I leave the office. Meanwhile, my teenage daughter becomes increasingly agitated. When I meet her at the restaurant, she is sitting alone, embarrassed, and almost in tears. Needless to say, the dinner is not pleasant.

Six months later, my partner enters my office to report the same problem with the same employee.

"Let's fire him," I say. "The problem has gone on long enough. Clearly, it cannot be corrected."

Most people procrastinate because they are not clear on their desired outcome (or on the steps that will generate this outcome). They do not have clarity. They procrastinate because they do not know what they want, so they do not know what behavior will take them to their desired goal.

When a person procrastinates on a problem, he will likely be stuck in a depressing mess of one problem after another. And like dominos falling, the problem will get worse rather than better. By failing to call my daughter, I hurt my daughter's feelings and created an unpleasant evening. By failing to address my human relations problem, I might have unnecessarily fired an employee who could have been saved.[22]

By finding clarity about who you want to be and how you want things to happen, you are often able to avoid the repercussions of procrastination. Imagine how this problem looks today with the assistance of clarity and Quadrant Thinking.

At half past five, I realize I will be late for the dinner I scheduled with my daughter. Because I have clearly defined the goals I want as a parent, I know that I want to treat my teenage daughter with respect and help her become a respectful adult. I call her in advance and apologize for my tardiness, and I ask her if she minds making an adjustment by pushing our dinner back fifteen minutes. She agrees.

My partner enters my office to tell me about a problem with one of my employees. Though I feel pressure to complete my paperwork before leaving town, I recognize that taking immediate steps to correct employee problems benefits everyone. To honor the business values I have established through clarity planning, I decide to address this elephant immediately. I ask if my partner and human resources director can call my cell phone in thirty minutes. I finish my paperwork and get in my car. My partner and the human resources director call my cell phone while I am driving to meet my daughter.

---

22 Attrition costs a business at least 25 percent of the employee's salary and, when considering lost production, as much as 200 percent of a person's salary. No matter which way you slice it, it ain't cheap!

We agree that the problem is imminent and needs to be addressed, setting specific targets that the employee must reach to keep his job. My partner and I delegate responsibility to the human resources director as I pull into the restaurant. Instead of being fifteen minutes late, I am right on time. I have completed my paperwork and addressed the elephant. My daughter is entering the parking lot at the same time. She hugs me, and we chat about our day.

When I return from my trip, I am astonished by my problem employee's change of behavior. He is cheerful, meets deadlines, and has quickly jumped from a below-average employee to a priceless employee.

As I mentioned earlier, Quadrant Thinking is a tool that addresses multifaceted issues, small problems, and everything in between. Finding your elephants means that you do not procrastinate when issues present themselves. Instead, give yourself three options:

1.   Deal with it.
2.   Delegate it.
3.   Schedule it.

If I cannot immediately address a problem, or if someone equally competent can address the problem for me, I try to delegate it. But from time to time, I simply have more pressing issues that I must tend to, and no one can handle one of my elephants on my behalf. When this is the case, I take a moment to schedule it in my calendar.

The moral of the story is this: elephants do not go away, and the longer you ignore them, the more of a problem they become. If you ignore an elephant too long, you will quickly find out what it is like to walk through a pile of elephant dung.[23] Instead, confront the elephant and get it out of your office. To do that, you must have clarity.

---

23 According to Ellen James, who works for the Carnegie Museum of Natural History, an adult elephant produces up to three hundred pounds of dung a day.

FINDING YOUR ELEPHANTS
AND THE DECISION SWAMP.

BRAD SPENCER, PhD, identifies the "Decision Swamp" as that muddy pit that can trap a person if he is dealing with the symptoms of a problem instead of the actual problem.

Delores Hickey, my client whose family overspends, tries to solve her problem by taking out bank loans, making more money, and working harder. Delores believes her problem is that she has too little money. In fact, this is a symptom of the actual problem: she is not keeping her family on a budget, and her family is not aware that they live in a world of limited resources. So Delores jumps into the Decision Swamp, getting bogged down as her family cries, "More money! More money!"

We are all guilty of this. When we lack clarity, our solutions are not commensurate with the actual problem, so we find ourselves in a quicksand-like situation where the harder we work to solve the problem, the more the problem engulfs us.

Several years ago, my named partners and I were feeling increasingly aggravated because the junior partners were not contributing to the critical decisions being made around the office. Because we have clarity surrounding our long-term plan of transitioning the firm to the younger partners, we were disappointed that our partners were not showing initiative. We made a decision: we told them that **they** would determine the course of our business. We put the decision balls in their court.

They did nothing. And as a result, we were bogged down, for sure. Not only were we frustrated with our younger partners, but with nothing happening, we had marketing needs that were being unmet, as well as other mounting problems that were not being addressed.

In short, we perceived a problem, came up with a solution, and when the solution failed, we decided our junior partners were not capable of making decisions.

> **Perceived problem:** Younger partners do not contribute to the decision-making process.
>
> **Solution:** Force them to make decisions.
>
> **Outcome:** They did not make decisions.
>
> **Conclusion:** Our younger partners are not competent.

Yet this conclusion did not resonate with what we knew to be true. When they were in their element, these younger partners were stars. They excelled when it came to leading their own team members and clients. Their failures when it came to the overall direction of the business did not make sense.

I scratched my head for a while, and when that did not work, I turned to our behaviorist, Dr. Spencer.

"You are in the Decision Swamp," said Spencer, explaining that we were trying to correct a symptom when we did not have clarity around the problem.

By spending time finding clarity, we realized that our junior partners were strong team players. They could make, implement, and sustain strong decisions. But they did not think we would validate their decisions. Our junior partners did not believe that we were willing to listen to them and let them make decisions. In fact, they were more than capable, but they thought taking control of the company's direction was useless because we had ignored their suggestions in the past.

When we found clarity, we found that our perceived problem was actually a symptom. By soliciting feedback from our junior partners, we realized that the solution was not what we previously thought. Instead of forcing our junior partners to make decisions, we opened the lines of communication and incorporated their suggestions. By opening the lines of communication, the junior partners felt validated and were empowered to run the business, which successfully accomplished our desired outcome.

Actual problem:	Our junior partners did not feel listened to.
Symptom:	Younger partners did not contribute to the decision-making process.
Solution:	Open the lines of communication and stop second-guessing junior partners.
Outcome:	Junior partners assume their rightful role, feel listened to, and successfully run the business.[24]
Conclusion:	By validating the input from our younger partners, the named partners engage the junior partners, who feel more comfortable making decisions and suggesting changes.

Avoiding the Decision Swamp starts by making a simple adjustment to your thought process. Start by perceiving problems as symptoms. Instead of thinking she has too little money, Delores Hickey must shift the problem down one notch and realize her financial woes are a symptom of another problem.

THE DECISION SWAMP	AVOIDING THE DECISION SWAMP
Delores's perceived problem: I don't have enough money.	**Delores's actual problem:** Family is not working as an economic unit.
	Symptom: I don't have enough money.
Solution: Take out bank loans, work harder.	**Solution:** Clearly layout financial capacity. Enlist all to make choices. Hold **all** accountable.
Outcome: Year after year, I don't have enough money.	**Outcome:** Family starts to live within its means.
Conclusion: I don't have enough money.	**Conclusion:** Family saves money and likes each other again.

You will notice two things about the Decision Swamp. First, when a perceived problem is actually a symptom, the solution often leads to more problems. In my case, our frustration with our junior partners grew. In Delores's case, the hamster wheel keeps spinning as she is forced to work harder and harder to make ends meet.

By definition, the Decision Swamp is messy, and a person becomes

---

24 How do you think I had time to write this book?

tangled inside it, patching up one symptom before being forced to move on to another. When symptoms are addressed instead of problems, you are like the proverbial hamster on a wheel—a bunch of motion but no progress.

The second thing you will notice from the diagram on the previous page is that the direct relationship between problem and solution is not always apparent.

In Delores Hickey's case, the actual problem has nothing to do with whether the family has money. In fact, one of Delores's children is an artist who has been given a $200,000 budget for living expenses. In normal circumstances, any artist given a nearly-quarter-million-dollar budget would be happier than a kid in a candy store.

But Delores's children do not work, and they spend with gusto, which keeps her fighting and fighting to make more money. At the same time, the symptom keeps resurfacing, reinforcing Delores's suspicion that she needs to make more money. In fact, Delores should turn her focus inward to find clarity about what she really wants, and how the current situation fails to resonate with her values.

Tapping into your values.

IF YOU HAVE NO VALUES and no moral standards, you will have a hard time making decisions that keep you out of jail.

Personally, I want to stay out of jail. I suspect you do, too.[25]

---

[25] Read Jim Stovall's wildly bestselling book, *The Ultimate Gift*. After a good cry, you will get in touch with the importance of values. It is a quick read. Go ahead and read it. I'll wait.

Wielding your strengths.

Although identifying problems is a crucial step in the search for clarity, spending time accentuating and protecting the positives is equally important.

Think of it like this: a football team has both defense and offense. Consider problem identification and elimination your defensive squad. Identifying, protecting, and wielding your strengths are your offense. You will need your star quarterback connecting with a running back to win the game!

I once had a client who owned a bakery. The bakery's main lines were low-carb products of all sorts: bagels, scones, sliced bread, and reheatable pancakes. The baker had a flourishing niche market and relied heavily on a particular specialty flour.

When the supplier was suddenly unable to continue producing the flour, the bakery business came to a near halt. Profits were down, customers were unhappy, and the bakery still has been unable to cobble together enough specialty flour to match its previous output.

By relying too heavily on one supplier and not envisioning a future where the supplier might go out of business, the bakery was caught off guard and had to go on the defensive. The bakery could have prepared for a snag in the supply chain had it been on the offensive, protecting its strengths (the business's livelihood) by researching other potential sources for this important ingredient.

When envisioning the future, pay attention to the core elements that bring you success. These are included in your strengths. In the case of the bakery, one of the strengths was the use of this specialized flour.

Protecting your strengths is critical. Strengths constitute your confidence. Your strengths will give you the confidence to discover hidden problems instead of evading them. Your strengths represent the confidence that gives you the ability to take advantage of opportunities and protect yourself from dangers. Your strengths stop you from standing in front of danger like a deer in headlights. By giving you confidence, your strengths simultaneously give you tools you can use to find clarity and later develop, implement, and sustain solutions. Your strengths will help you plan for various futures, be flexible about the paths you choose, and recognize opportunities others cannot.

Knowing that specialized flour was the one thing that differentiated the bakery, the owners should have examined what could sap that element of strength. Not having the flour certainly did. A bit of planning could have assured other sources. The strength was not in the bakery's ability to receive the flour from **that** particular manufacturer, but rather to receive that flour from **any** manufacturer. Looking at the strength, understanding it, and determining what could void its power is a critical part of clarity planning.

Finding your elephants, even if you do not have an M.B.A.

Identifying your particular elephants means asking the right questions before making a decision.

Instead of playing "Whack-a-Mole" as you address issues as they pop up, spend the majority of your time in the Clarity Quadrant asking yourself introspective questions. This is where values come in. The guideposts to clarity have to do with the values that resonate with you. A plan that is not grounded in affirming values you hold dear is a plan that is made of cardboard rather than of sturdy timber.

Through a series of questions, Dan Sullivan uses "The D.O.S. Conversation®,"[26] a worksheet that identifies a person's **D**angers (What keeps you up at night?), **O**pportunities (What excites you?), and **S**trengths (Where does your confidence lie?).

Business planners and strategists use a similar tool—the SWOT Analysis—to find a business or person's **S**trengths, **W**eaknesses, **O**pportunities, and **T**hreats. Combined with an assessment of your values, a D.O.S.™ or SWOT Analysis helps you answer these questions: *Who am I? What would my ideal life/business/relationship look like?*

My accountancy firm is more than a transactional service provider. In addition to tax advice, we also offer legacy planning (which might include

---

26 The D.O.S. Conversation® and D.O.S.™ are trademarks and copyrights owned by the Strategic Coach® Inc. All rights reserved. Used with written permission. www.strategiccoach.com.

estate planning, succession planning, or exit planning). When meeting with a client, we always start with one critical question:

| CRITICAL QUESTION |

"If we were meeting here three years from today— and you were to look back over those three years to today—what has to have happened during that period, both personally and professionally, for you to feel happy about your progress?"

This is what Dan Sullivan of the Strategic Coach® calls "The R-Factor Question®."[27]

This question is predicated on your values, and its motive is to uncover your goals. Consider which values the following answers might support:

- *My business will have self-sustaining systems, and I will have grown its net profits by 15 percent.* (values: entrepreneurialism, family/free time)

- *My legacy plan will include a $500,000 endowment to cancer research.* (values: science, philanthropy)

- *My children will have graduated from college and have started their own careers.* (values: education, independence, resourcefulness)

- *I will be stuffed by a taxidermist and preserved in the corner of my favorite museum.* (values: art, self-indulgence)

We then move on to ask four other questions:

1. *What are my **strengths**? What attributes, resources, and skills do I have? In what activities do I feel most confident?*

---

27 The R-Factor Question® is a trademark and copyright owned by the Strategic Coach® Inc. All rights reserved. Used with written permission. www.strategiccoach.com.

2. *What are my internal **weaknesses**? What keeps me awake at night? What are the things that would need to be eliminated in order for me to feel safe? What skills do I lack that intefere with my values? What attributes of mine might present obstacles to being happy?*

3. *What are the **opportunities** I have? What external conditions might help me realize and affirm my values?*

4. *What about the external **threats**? Are there outside conditions that might hinder achievement of my objective?*

Notice that by answering these questions, you have simultaneously created the skeleton of a strategic plan for your future. Your strategic plan looks to satisfy those long-term needs—both business and personal—that must be met for you to feel fulfilled.

Remember that in answering these questions, you should consider the moral implications of each one. What do your answers indicate about your values? Identifying and acknowledging your values makes conquering your elephants easier. If you know that you value education, and an elephant walks into the room that threatens education, you are more prone to immediately remove it.

By answering these questions, you can then work to eliminate the dangers and fears, capitalize on opportunities and excitement, and preserve and enhance your confidence and strengths in the Solutions Quadrant.

In reaching clarity, the solutions to your everyday problems become manageable: by identifying what you want, you also identify what needs to be addressed, delegated, or removed from your life.

The path to clarity is usually not terribly complex as long as you keep in mind the elements discussed earlier and the questions. The answers can be as long or as short as you want, so long as they are SMART: **S**pecific, **M**easurable, **A**ctionable, **R**elevant, and **T**ime-Bounded.

We will discuss this further in Quadrant Two.

KEY POINTS

In any problem, large or small, clarity planning answers one critical question: *What does the ideal outcome look like?* The Clarity Quadrant focuses on answering this question and setting a vision from which you will later define your action plan. See the Quadrant Thinking Conductor for a step-by-step process for attaining clarity.

Clarity planning takes effort, and pain is swell. Attaining clarity is no easy task. In fact, it might be painful. To move toward your vision, you must accept pain as part of the process, commit to enduring the pain, and be patient. No one has ever trained for and completed a 26.2-mile race during a lunch break. But pushing through the pain and patiently moving forward will be more than worth it if you truly want to achieve a goal.

Believe in a bigger future. Setting goals that are motivating, and then looking forward to these goals, and believing that they are possible, will drastically increase your chances of reaching clarity.

Clarity is the enemy of the status quo. If you are unhappy with the current state of affairs, reaching clarity will endanger the status quo by identifying a solution that moves you in a new direction.

Focus on the goal, not the distractions. Distractions come in the form of people, setbacks, fear of failure, or even fear of success. Focusing on the goal, and having absolute clarity that you want to achieve this goal, makes the distractions irrelevant.

Finding your elephants and procrastination. If you ignore an elephant for too long, you will quickly find out what it is like to walk through a pile of elephant dung. Instead, confront the elephant immediately and get it out of your office by either dealing with it, delegating it to someone else, or scheduling time to address it.

Finding your elephants and the Decision Swamp. When we lack clarity, our solutions are often incommensurate with the actual problems. We find ourselves in quicksand-like situations where the harder we work to solve a problem the more it engulfs us. The solutions do not lead to the desired outcome. To avoid this, try making a simple adjustment to your thought process. When dealing with a problem, consider that the obvious and perceived problem might be a symptom of another problem. By uncovering the actual problem, solutions can be matched with the desired outcome.

Tapping into your values. Read *The Ultimate Gift* by Jim Stovall to get in touch with your values, which are critical to reaching clarity.

Wielding your strengths. When moving toward clarity, remember that uncovering obstacles is only part of the process. You must also identify, protect, and wield your strengths. What are the core elements that make you or your business unique? How can these be leveraged, protected, and preserved?

Finding your elephants, even if you do not have an M.B.A. Ask yourself The R-Factor Question®, created by Dan Sullivan of The Strategic Coach®. Predicated on your values, The R-Factor Question® addresses your strengths, weaknesses, opportunities, and threats, and creates the beginning of a strategic plan for you or your business.

QUADRANT TWO

SOLUTIONS

Quadrant Two | SOLUTIONS

SATIRIST AMBROSE BIERCE ONCE DEFINED "plan" as "to bother about the best method of accomplishing an accidental result." I take Bierce to mean that we spend too much time worrying about what we are going to do when what we do seldom leads us to the outcome we think it will. With all due respect to Bierce,[1] the truth is somewhat different: because most of us do not know where we want to go (we do not have clarity), we do not plan the appropriate steps that will take us there.

In Quadrant Two of *Say Hello to the Elephants,* we focus on the solutions.[2] The goals you define in Quadrant One specify where you want to go; your solution tells you how you are going to get there. The Clarity Quadrant is the pilot's destination, and the Solution Quadrant is the flight plan.

Your solution names the specific actions that will lead to the achievement of a goal. If your goal is to implement your legacy plan, your specific actions might be to meet with a legacy planning advisor, transfer your assets into the appropriate trusts, and create conditions that direct your heirs' behavior. Or, if your goal is to increase your company's bottom line by 15 percent during the next fiscal year, your actions might be to hire a new salesperson or recoup your freight costs from your customers.

Why is it necessary to define a solution? The question answers itself when rephrased as: Why is it necessary to figure out how to achieve your goals? It is not enough to know what you want. You need to identify how to get it, which is not always obvious. Moreover, by explicitly defining what actions you will

---

[1] Not necessarily the most positive fellow to have ever lived, Bierce was nicknamed Bitter Bierce. I bet this really irked his parents, who gave all thirteen of their children first names that began with the letter "A."

[2] Let's stop being part of the problem.

take to achieve your goals, you will find it increasingly difficult to delude yourself about your commitment to achieving these goals.

Each element of your solution must name a **S**pecific, **M**easurable, **A**ctionable, **R**elevant, and **T**ime-bounded action you have to perform.

In business-speak, this is called the process of setting "SMART goals." It works like this: if your goal is to lose weight, merely listing, "Go to the gym regularly," is not enough. Your solution must detail exactly what actions the goal entails. The more room you leave for interpretation, the more you risk interpreting yourself out of pursuing your goals. As such, the solution to your goal must be SMART:

Goal: To lose weight.

SMART Action Plan:

- **S**pecific: Exercise at the gym,

- **M**easurable: Four times a week,

- **A**ctionable: So that I can lose fifteen pounds,

- **R**elevant: And support my goal of working another twenty years,

- **T**ime-bounded: Within three months.

Solution: Excercise at the gym four times a week so that I can lose fifteen pounds within three months and support my goal of working another twenty years.

In the following chapters, I provide some guidelines for creating a proper solution.

Determining the actions that will lead to your desired results often takes research. In some cases, you will not know the action items required to achieve a goal. For instance, you might have the goal of planning your estate, but have no clue as to what this involves. In such a case, your solution will be to consult an expert (in this case, an estate planner, who can help you create a full solution). During this quadrant, we discuss the proper method of finding trusted advisors so that your solution addresses your overarching vision, as determined in Quadrant One.

You may find that when you try to define your solution, you sometimes go blank—you cannot imagine what actions would lead to the fulfillment of the goal.[3] Often times, this means you need to go back to the Clarity Quadrant and make sure you have been clear and specific about where your destination is and what your goals are.

Solutions, like goals, must be revamped from time to time. For more on this, see Quadrant Four: Sustainability. For now, let's delve further into Quadrant Two.

---

3 *Why?* can be like peeling an onion, trying to find real reasons that are deeply hidden under many layers. The real reasons can make you cry.

OBSTACLES ARE STEPPING STONES
THAT NARROW THE SOLUTION.

WHEN PEOPLE TALK ABOUT GOALS they cannot achieve, they usually cite a hailstorm of obstacles: they cannot increase profits because the economy is in the dumps; they cannot lose weight because they do not have time to go to the gym; they cannot pursue their dreams because they lack resources.

Dr. Brad Spencer teaches that there are two kinds of obstacles that block our path to success: some are blocks that we can do nothing about. He calls these "World Blocks," and they are obstacles that are based on circumstances beyond control. But by in large, the majority of obstacles are "Personal Blocks," and these can be addressed and eliminated. In fact, overcoming these obstacles brings us one step closer to achieving our goals.

By shifting your perspective, you can begin to see that most obstacles are milestones that represent achievement. Planning to eliminate obstacles clearly progresses a person one step closer to a goal. In this context, obstacles are not barriers but welcoming mileposts.

Let's use my long-term business planning for Rose, Snyder & Jacobs as an example.

When I started my business, I had one specific goal: to feed my wife and myself. As my family grew to include two children, my goal transitioned to have my business as long as necessary to support my children through college. Now I have had my business for thirty years and my youngest child is a junior in high school. My goal may be within sight, but I am not done. My goal has now changed; I want to continue working for another thirty years.

| GOAL |
Continue my business for thirty more years

As we learned from Quadrant One, setting this goal makes the obstacle and the desired result obvious. For the past several years, I have worried that I do not have the stamina to maintain my schedule. My mind is willing, but is my body? I have flagging stamina. I tend to overeat, and I do not exercise.

| OBSTACLE |
Flagging stamina

Instead of deciding that I cannot possibly achieve my goal because I lack stamina, I can identify this obstacle and create a solution that increases my chance of success: among other things, my solution must include a plan to improve my stamina to be healthy, vibrant, and active for thirty years and beyond so that I can work fifty hours a week and enjoy the time I am not working.

My solution could ignore my flagging stamina, but this would stop me from reaching my goal. When identifying a solution, consider the over-arching goals and corresponding dangers and obstacles. For instance, what lifestyle changes can I make to improve my stamina? If I am eating poorly, not exercising, and working arduous hours, all of those habits are contributing to my poor stamina. In considering all of this information, the solution becomes easier to identify, and the elimination of the obstacle becomes a stepping stone toward my goal.

If I can make small changes, I should see a gradual improvement in my stamina over time. I can be more selective in what I order for lunch, walk eighteen holes when I golf, or hire additional staff and streamline some of my processes to cut the number of hours I work. I can engage in a workout regimen to protect my heart and comfortably carry my weight. I know I will never want to be a marathon runner, but if I implement these concrete steps to address each bad habit, and then review my stamina in another six months, I am much more likely to overcome this obstacle.

Are there any other elephants I need to consider with respect to long-term business planning? I know that one of my goals for retirement is to have a flourishing business that provides income even while retired.

That said, I foresee an obstacle. My goal will be squashed if I do not have a competent team to whom I can transition responsibilities. I need to embark in a partner development plan to make sure that I have competent managers so that I can enjoy my retirement years.

| SOLUTION |

**Implement concrete steps to improve stamina.
Develop a team of upper and middle-level managers
who will be in place to sustain business when I leave.**

My other partners and I are thinking about ways to address this elephant far in advance because putting together a workable management team can take years. I need to work with my current young partners and managers on developing training programs, solidifying our mission statement, and identifying current employees who might be interested in the management track. I need to increase revenue to hire additional managers. I might want to hire an independent management specialist to help me develop a five or ten-year plan to achieve all these important steps. Regardless, this solution would have been impossible without 100 percent clarity about my long-term goals and vision. Instead, attacking the individual obstacles brings the ultimate goal closer as every obstacle is overcome.

Take, for instance, Mitch, my client who was unwilling to implement his estate plan for years on end. The minute Mitch found clarity, the obstacle became much more obvious, and Mitch was willing to sign into effect his estate planning documents. It was not enough to simply plan to divide his assets and avoid taxes; Mitch's solution had to include a plan to transfer values, the obstacle that represented a milestone in Mitch's planning progress.

The obstacle elimination phase should always include these three steps:

1. Identify the goal, from which you can realize your objectives.

2. Identify the obstacles to reaching this goal, a process that will help you narrow and focus your solutions.

3. Identify the solutions to eliminate your obstacles.

Do not be fooled into thinking the obstacle-elimination phase will be automatic. After identifying obstacles, you must work to conscientiously eliminate them. This will be a continuous process. It may be that after you eliminate one looming obstacle, another obstacle that was in the background will push its way to the front. When you eliminate **that** one, **another** will rear its ugly head, and so on.

Just know that a finite number of obstacles will present themselves. Eventually, all obstacles will be addressed. Goal achieved!

SAUSAGE IS SUBJECTIVE.

RECENTLY, I HAD AN EPIPHANY while ordering dinner with one of the partners at my firm, Rebecca. We were considering the toppings for our pizza when I declared my love for sausage. I assumed Rebecca would wholeheartedly agree. Who doesn't love sausage?[4]

Instead of nodding in agreement, Rebecca looked perplexed. She was searching for words, and she finally said, "Sausage is subjective."

I realized immediately that Rebecca was right: some sausage is sweet; some is spicy. Some is pork, some is chicken, and some is beef. Some is even duck! One cannot simply make a blanket statement such as, "I love sausage." Depending on individual tastes, most people do not unequivocally love sausage.

Such is the case of solutions. Your solution must resonate with your tastes. What tastes good to someone else might not work for you.[5]

When considering solutions to complicated legal, tax, business, or personal issues with an advisor, be sure to ask questions to ensure that you understand how solutions are designed and whether they are the right fit for you. Remember that more than one path will take you to the same mountaintop.

Communication between you and your team members is key. Do not assume you and your advisor are on the same page. Instead, make sure everyone involved has absolute clarity about what the goal is, and then discuss all the different ways to achieve the goal. Remember that solutions should be

4 PETA, that's who!
5 Blood sausage.

based on individual preferences. Make sure your advisor knows to present multiple solutions because sausage is subjective.

| CRITICAL QUESTION |

Do I completely understand the solution that is being proposed? If I completely understand a solution, I will know the answers to these questions:

- **What is it?**
- **How is it applicable?**
- **Why does it work?**
- **What can go wrong?**
- **Who must be involved?**
- **How much does it cost to implement?**
- **How much does it cost to sustain?**
- **What must be done to sustain it?**

Let's say you want to start up your own sausage factory because you love sausage so much you would like to have it available at all times. You tell your advisor, Rebecca, about your plans. With Rebecca's help, you learn all about the process of making sausage. You learn that selecting ingredients is one of the primary steps toward making good sausage. You ask your advisor to help you find the right ingredients.

But what's this? Rebecca brings you vegetarian ingredients, including an assortment of tofu, seitan,[6] nuts, legumes, soya protein, and vegetables. Rebecca assumes that because you live in vegetable-crazy Los Angeles, you will want to appeal to a vegan and vegetarian clientele.

As a result, you will have sausage, but not at all the kind you want. You want meat! Though Rebecca had the best intentions and was trying to help you identify a niche market and reach your goal, she started out on the wrong foot because she did not have the correct information.

By discussing all of the different solutions and identifying those that resonate with your values, you will be that much closer to owning and operating a delicious meat-loving sausage factory.

---

6 Whatever that is.

To achieve your desired results, you must always understand how and why a solution meets your goals. With the proper understanding, you can accurately monitor your progress as you move forward.

Okay, so Rebecca now knows you are a carnivore, and you now have exactly the kind of ingredients your stomach craves. The next step toward having a fully functional, operating sausage factory is the grinding and thermal processing. Learning the ins and outs of this process is imperative. If grinding and thermal processing is done incorrectly, the sausage will not be true sausage—and no one, not even your mother, will want to buy product from this factory.

Without fully understanding how your solution works, you will be unable to measure your progress and fully gauge how much closer you are to achieving the goal.

To be sure, there will be surprises along the way, but expecting the unexpected will help you address obstacles. Part of being able to deal with the unexpected is asking yourself or your advisor the following question: *What could go wrong?* If the grinding and thermal processing is not done correctly in a sausage factory, everything could go wrong. Knowing what could go wrong means knowing what can be done to prevent unnecessary obstacles.

If running a sausage factory truly is your goal (hey, anything is possible), then you would quickly become acquainted with food-safety guidelines. You and your employees would learn to wash your hands regularly, keep the equipment clean, keep the meat as cold as possible, and so on and so forth. If you failed to implement the appropriate solutions, you would end up on the evening news due to all the people who hurled after eating your product. That would be bad.

Having gone through the grinding and thermal processing of the sausage (and you will thank me for sparing the details), you still have many benchmarks. Before embarking on your journey, you should be intimately familiar with the steps you will take, and you should evaluate whether you can and want to complete each step—information that is far better to have in advance than in the middle of a journey.

This is where your advisor plays a crucial role. She must be sure to adequately and accurately explain each step in the solution you have chosen.

Rebecca, for instance, should tell you that if you are to run a success-ful factory, you are going to need variety: beef jerky, hot pickle cure jerky, sweet Italian sausage, dried beef, braunschweiger, haggis, blood sausage, Italian hot sausage, German grits, fresh pork sausage, venison garlic sausage, Polish sausage, Lar's super garlic sausage, venison summer sausage, smoked bratwurst, smoked turkey and pork sausage, and sausage sausage.[7]

When you consider a solution, one of two things should happen: either the solution will feel wrong, or it will feel right. Maybe you simply want to make the perfect sausage for your pizza, and by considering all the solutions, you realize that starting your own sausage factory is not necessarily the solu-tion that achieves your goal.

Or maybe you are fired up and ready to go! You cannot wait to get started and look forward to having a party for the grand opening where people show up, look around, and say, "Wow, this place is a real sausage factory."

If that is the case, if you are fired up and ready to go, then you know you are not going to be able to do it all by yourself. You will need more than your advisor. You will need an army of trusted friends, colleagues, patrons, and workers. The question to ask is this: *Who must be involved?*

Knowing the steps other people need to take is as important as knowing what you must do. Putting together the right team is a critical part of this process. With your advisor's help, you can choose capable people before you even get started.

Another important question to ask when exploring various solutions is this: *What will be the cost of this solution?* Your advisor should be able to help with the answer to this question, which will be weighed against the solu-tion's benefits. Obviously, if the costs outweigh the benefits, you need to find another solution.

If your sausage factory is going to cost $1,400,000, you need to know ahead of time if it is going to generate $50,000. If your advisor presents plans that cost more than they net, something is amiss.

One of the most important factors is considering what the alternatives are to your solution. Your advisor should never say, "This is how it is done,"

---

7 Rebecca is a little like Bubba.

or "This is how we are going to do it." Because there is rarely, if ever, only one solution, you should always have options. Rather than locking into a concrete plan, your advisor should approach solutions with the following in mind: *This is one of the ways we can accomplish the goal, but there are other roads to explore as well.*

By thoroughly considering other paths, you might choose the best of many appropriate solutions, giving you the confidence to know why you chose this sausage instead of that sausage.

Always remember: sausage is subjective. When you understand the thermal and grinding process, as well as when to serve mustard and horse-radish instead of grilled onions, you will know which variety of sausage is right for you. If you do not understand, you might find yourself with duck on your pizza, or soy chicken, which even members of PETA will admit is gross.

THE ARTICHOKE THEORY.

IN WORKING TOWARD ACHIEVEMENT of a certain goal, always remember to keep it simple. The steps should always be broken into small, achievable milestones.

Imagine building a new two-story house. In an effort to save a few dollars, your contractor talks you into having only two steps between the first and second floors. You may have saved money in the short run, but you now require mountain climbing gear to get to your bedroom. It sounded like a good idea at the time, but when thought through, the original plan of fifteen steps to reach the second floor is a much better idea.[8]

The smaller the steps of the solution, the simpler things get, and the more likely the outcome is to be favorable. I call this the Artichoke Theory.

Let's imagine that you have reached clarity about your tax planning. Your advisor tells you that you must create a sale to an intentionally defective grantor trust[9] to achieve your goal of shifting wealth to your children. Your advisor goes on to explain the technical details of intentionally defective grantor trusts, using industry jargon and legalese you do not understand. Your eyes glaze over, and you start thinking about what you will eat for lunch. When it comes time to implement the solution, you fail because you have no idea what your advisor is talking about.

---

8 Especially if you suffer from vertigo.

9 Huh?

Now imagine that your goal remains the same: shifting wealth to your children. Your accountant explains the solution as follows:

1.   With the help of your advisors, establish a trust that will be recognized for estate tax purposes but not income tax purposes.

2.   Gift money into that trust.

3.   Working with your advisors, use the trust monies to purchase an appreciating asset from you and your spouse so the trust owns the asset.

Though both solutions are identical, you can see which is simpler. Though you might have questions about the second solution, you know you can achieve it.

In other words, you should eat an elephant the same way you eat an artichoke: one leaf at a time.[10]

Imagine your main goal as an umbrella. If you are to keep things simple, then all matters relating to your main goal should fall under this umbrella. While working toward your goal, stop and ask yourself: *Is what I am doing right now directly related to reaching my main goal?* The answer should always be a resounding *yes* if you are keeping things simple. If the answer is *no*, then you are only making things more difficult for yourself.

| CRITICAL QUESTION |
Is what I am doing right now directly related to reaching my main goal?

Suppose there was a man named Erik, and Erik had a goal of climbing Mount Everest. His goal was clear: to reach the summit of the world's highest mountain. He knew a great deal of planning would go into making it all the way. He fully expected to one day be atop Mount Everest and anticipated the results of such an accomplishment. For Erik, the results, among other things,

---

10 With melted butter.

would be an incredible sense of human achievement and humility, a certain amount of positive notoriety, and a stronger feeling of overall self-confidence in any future endeavors. Erik welcomed these results, so he began to carefully plan his adventure.

With hundreds of things on his "to do" list, Erik knew that if he did not keep each task simple, he would never complete his list. Tackling them all at once would be like trying to surf a tidal wave: chaotic and ultimately futile. But by keeping things simple, approaching each requirement individually, Erik eventually got through his list: he did all of the appropriate research; Erik did one practice climb after another; he exercised and ate well to keep his blood pressure and cholesterol down; he acquired all the necessary equipment; he tested the equipment in advance. Each of these activities fell directly under the umbrella of "Climbing Mount Everest."

Imagine what would have happened if these steps were not broken into small chunks. Likely, he would have never reached the summit, distracted by activities outside the umbrella. Erik might want to write a book about his planned experiences, and he could have spent time cutting a book deal instead of tackling his "Climbing Mount Everest" list. While this is related to Mount Everest, it does not fit directly under the umbrella, and focusing on this could have been debilitating.

But Erik kept things simple by focusing on the goal at hand. This is why on May 25, 2001, at age thirty-two, Erik Weihenmeyer reached the top of Mount Everest.

By the way, Erik is blind.

Erik knew that keeping things simple was the only way to avoid complications, and this holds true regardless of whether you are trying to climb Everest or land a great job.

Be aware that simple is not the same as easy. "Simple" means that the actions you take relate directly to your overall goal. They should be small and directly connected, but they are not necessarily easy.

In fact, a solution that seems too easy should raise a red flag, especially in the complex world of taxation, business, and law. When a solution seems too easy, trust your gut and ask your advisors to explain why, in laymen's terms, a solution will get you to your goal. If a solution defies your logic after a thorough hearing, do not implement it. Remember that you, not your advisors, have to live with the results of your planning. Stepping into a solution is not always easy, or even painless, but you should always know in simple terms what the solution is, how it relates to your goal, and why it will work.

In the early 2000s, a number of people were presented with the "opportunity" to buy a house. Many of these people did not qualify for conventional home loans. Traditionally, borrowers had to qualify for financing by proving they could reasonably pay the monthly payments through their income, assets, or savings, but some lenders created an "opportunity" for borrowers who did not qualify: lenders decided to approve loans for people who might not make ends meet once their monthly payments began to increase due to rising interest rates, or due to the expiration of teaser rates designed to create a climate where introductory rates were artificially low. But those borrowers applying for the loans, and those lenders approving the loans, unfortunately overlooked this little detail.

The solution did not match the goal:

Borrower's Goal:	Buy a home I can afford.
Borrower's "Solution:"	Apply for a loan that I will not be able to afford after five years unless I win the lottery.
Lender's Goal:	Provide loans for people who can afford to pay them.
Lender's "Solution:"	Give subprime mortgages to people who can barely afford to make payments. When they lose their homes, I will lose my income.

The "opportunity" was a shortcut, and it sounded easy enough. *After all,* thought the lender, *the house will keep increasing in value. If the buyer cannot pay the mortgage, he can always sell it at a gain, and we can get paid.* The lenders, in particular, should have known better. Aware of the cyclical nature of the real estate industry, they should have anticipated the inevitable: the homes dropped in value.

It should have also seemed too easy to those homebuyers with poor credit and low incomes. The homebuyer failed to think ahead.

Too many failed to ask for clarity. The lenders forgot to say, "When the mortgage rate adjusts in a little while, those people will be unable to meet their financial commitments and leave us without a way to recoup our losses if the homes do not increase in value!"

The borrowers forgot to ask: "What can go wrong?"

Though seemingly easy, this proved to be a complex formula. The simple formula would have been "loan money to people who can make their payments." And for homeowners, this simple formula would have been, "borrow money only if we can afford to make the payments." And had certain people stuck to this simple formula, a lot of people would be a lot happier these days.

Often keeping things simple can be easier said than done. Human nature is to take the shortcut every now and then, to get drawn into something complicated, and to feel stress as a result of these complications. The more anxious we feel, the more we lose our focus, and the less simple our strategies and ability to achieve our goals.

So how can we continue to stay focused and keep things simple? The answer itself is simple: river rafting. The teamwork required for river rafting is applicable to any endeavor in real life. The raging river offers all team members its tumultuous scenarios. Success and failure are determined by how we work together as a team, and by how well we work individually. The work itself is simple. When you are on a roaring rapid, your mind clears. You row in the direction you are supposed to, or you find yourself underwater. It's simple: do or die. Paddle or fall out of the boat. We continue to stay focused by refusing to lose sight of our main goal.

The philosophy of successful river rafting—the clarity and simplicity of what *must* be done to stay in the boat—can be applied to your goal and solution. Maybe you want to start a new business. The challenges and difficulties you would face along the way—and there would be many—are like the unpredictable torrents of water taking you in all sorts of directions. As long as you keep things simple by remembering the prime objective, you will maximize your probability of survival, whatever twists and turns come your way.

Of course, sometimes our plans do not work out exactly as expected. No matter how long we have planned, whatever scenarios we have anticipated, life throws us a curveball. When life throws us a curveball, keeping things simple becomes most important. If panic sets in when we are faced with unanticipated challenges, that panic only serves to muddy the waters. Already complicated situations then become even more complicated.

SLOW DOWN. YOU ARE IN A HURRY.

PURSUING YOUR MOST MEANINGFUL GOALS is imminent, and once you have achieved clarity, you will likely feel a surge of energy to quickly accomplish the goals. But when something is important, you must slow down, focus on the solutions, or risk making rash decisions.

I know a film producer who carries enormous responsibilities on her shoulders. Because of her job description, she certainly could be voted "Most Likely to Implode in a Fit of Panic." But she never does.

When I first met her, she was producing a mini-series. All of the locations were selected, the sets built, the crew hired. The series was missing only two things: the female star and the male star.

This was kind of a problem on the last Friday prior to filming. The director's agent called the producer and told her his client was getting nervous.

Without hesitation, the producer calmly responded to the agent, "Tell him to get un-nervous."

For the producer, the solution to this major problem was simple. Scripts would be sent to actors over the weekend, and the mini-series would find its cast. To the producer's assistant, this sounded impossible, and he was panicked. The producer knew that if her assistant was not calm and collected, the weekend plans would not come to fruition. The assistant would make mistakes collating scripts, or he would neglect to hire a courier, or forget to make an important phone call.

"Slow down," the producer told her assistant. "We are in a hurry."

He took a deep breath and realized that forty-eight hours was more than enough to find two starving actors willing to play the lead roles in a mini-series broadcast on network television.

And it was.

When faced with an important goal, slow down. Because you are in a hurry, take deep breaths and remind yourself to get un-nervous. Only then will you have the wherewithal to address obstacles, make rational decisions, and move your plans forward.

THE LAW OF UNINTENDED CONSEQUENCES.

JERRY AND ALLAN ARE EACH LEADERS in their industry. In 2004, they both attended a trade symposium held at a convention center in a large metropolitan area. Both intended to network, though Jerry wanted to have a good time. One night, Jerry and Allan attended an industry banquet and mixer. Allan made an effort to meet as many people as possible. He brought pictures of his wife and children and talked about his community activities, the outdoor sports he enjoyed, and his goals for his business. He was genuinely interested in getting to know people and hoped they would remember him later. He held a drink in his hand most of the night, but he rarely drank from it.

Jerry drank heavily. Although he was not obnoxious, he was not in the mood to chat about his wife and kids, or even really his business. This was his chance to get away from all of that. A group of traveling nurses was staying at the same hotel. Jerry invited them into the convention hall after the banquet and started buying drinks.

After introducing himself to as many people as possible, Allan was tired but satisfied with his evening. He politely excused himself, explaining that it was time to call his wife and children. He retired early and spent the remainder of the night in his hotel room.

Jerry closed down the bar with a few of the nurses and some other men attending the symposium. When he finally went to his room, he did not go alone.

Two years later, a group of venture capitalists were deciding what to do with some investment funds. Both Jerry's and Allan's names came across the table. A few members of the group had been at the trade symposium. They had met Allan and liked him. They could remember him talking about his wife and kids. They remembered that he enjoyed mountain biking.

Most of them remembered Jerry only vaguely. One of the women remembered that he had been wearing a wedding ring but had spent most of the night with some female nurses. One of the men had been in the group at the bar with the nurses and remembered that Jerry had not left alone that night.

Their concern with Jerry was not based on morality, though some of the members certainly frowned on his behavior. But from a purely business perspective, the venture capitalists were out to make money, not to judge moral worthiness. However, Jerry's failure to use the symposium as a networking opportunity made an impression on the venture capitalists. If Jerry was unable to make the most of this symposium, what would he do with their investment? The venture capitalists knew that messiness in one area tended to spill over into business areas as well. They went with Allan.

All conduct has unintended consequences. However inconvenient a truism it may be, the unintended consequences of negative or purposeless behavior are inevitably negative; on the other hand, positive conduct, or conduct that works toward a clear purpose, is inevitably rewarded with positive consequences, even when the consequences are unintended.

One of the goals of this chapter is that you accept that unintended consequences are manageable—even positive—if your conduct is pointed toward a clear goal in all respects. The other goal of this chapter is that you become more intentional in your causation of and preparation for the unintended consequences in your life and your business.

In any interaction, if your goals are clear and your direction defined, you will benefit from positive unintended consequences. These will almost always have more meaning and be larger in impact and reward than the original intended goal. This is not to say that the goal was not important, but that the outcomes are like happy dolphins swimming around a ship. You don't have to whistle or net them in. They just come along.

With clarity, your unintended consequences become what Dan Sullivan of the Strategic Coach® calls "strategic byproducts" of your planned conduct. Strategic byproducts are always positive because the intentionality of planning, the purposefulness of goals, and the alignment of goals with values all create a solid base with which other positive things can attach. Even if you are not looking for these dolphins, they come to you because you are a positive magnet.

A wonderful example is Calvin, a highly successful litigation attorney in his state. Calvin places an emphasis on physical fitness. His partners are expected to maintain top-notch health, and this expectation is communicated all the way down to the administrative and support staff. All members of the firm are granted flexible hours when used for fitness. Reminders about the importance of fitness are distributed on a regular basis, and the firm hosts seminars about health and nutrition.

Calvin explains that whenever the firm is in trial, the benefits of fitness are immediately apparent. Inevitably, the opposing attorneys lack the stamina and have difficulty handling the long hours and stress attendant with trial. Calvin and his partners, on the other hand, are able to remain fresh, fit, and focused however long the hours or pressing the stress.

No one sets out to lack stamina or to fall vulnerable to the physical ravages of stress, but these are unintended consequence of the negative conduct of failing to care for oneself: not exercising, overeating, drinking too heavily, smoking cigarettes, and the like.

Those who do act to increase their physical health, whatever their intended consequence may be, enjoy innumerable unintended consequences of healthy bodies: increased longevity, the ability to fight disease and sickness, decreased stress, and more happiness.

Unbeknownst to Calvin, one of his legal secretaries had a sister who was the business editor of the major publication in his region. Over drinks with her sister, the legal secretary discussed how enlightened the law firm was with respect to their emphasis on fitness. One thing led to another, and the publication ran a feature story about Calvin's firm. Shortly thereafter, he was nominated for and won an award for being one of the top ten legal firms in the city. Resumes from lawyers and support team candidates came streaming in. The CEO of a major company called Calvin after reading the piece and hired him on the spot. A solution that was intended to promote stamina so that Calvin and his firm could support a long and stressful trial schedule ultimately generated a pool of great candidates to accommodate a large and unexpected growth in the firm's client base. Strategic byproduct to say the least!

In addition to physical fitness, some of the key examples of positive conduct include responsible social behavior, which can lead to increased business; kindness toward others, which in turn leads to stronger relationships and more referrals; financial responsibility, which opens doors to unexpected business investments; and integrity. I believe every march to a solution creates strategic byproducts.

Let us think back to Jerry, the partier who attended the conference. Some of the unintended consequences of irresponsible social conduct include divorce and division of assets, isolation from children, loss of respect from colleagues and associates, health risks, and unplanned pregnancies. Jerry's conduct has already cost him investors, but that could be the least of his worries.

Let us contrast that with Allan. Allan did not refrain from spending time with the nurses because he thought it might cost him investors, but because it would violate his personal moral code. The unintended consequences, or the strategic byproducts, of Allan's positive conduct included the respect of his colleagues, protection of his assets, a healthy bond with his wife and children, and the trust of those who would invest in his endeavors.

And what about the unintended consequences of the lenders who failed to qualify their borrowers, and the borrowers who failed to refuse a deal that was clearly too good to be true? This lack of consciousness set the tables spinning: the unintended consequences include lost jobs, lost homes, lost lives, lost fortunes, and major legislation that is going to cost the country billions of dollars. Every single player had a little bit of larceny in him, didn't he? No one is clean.

An example of how important kindness can be in ensuring positive unintended consequences comes from my biggest client, a man who runs his business by values but has not always planned well for the lean times. During the land recession of the 1980s, his family found itself in an unenviable position of being very strapped for cash. However, it turned out that one of the most important assets this man had was his history of kindness, generosity, and integrity. Those values had been reflected in his interactions with his most important business colleagues as well as the secretaries who helped him. So when this man ran into trouble, and it was big trouble, his strategic byproduct of honoring these values was that nobody in the world wanted to see him fail. The banks were demanding payment, but the community stepped in, introduced him to investors who helped him find new lenders, partners, and potential investors. Because he was intentionally a good person, everyone around him was pulling for him, including his competitors! Even his bankers gave him a bit more time to right the ship. As he was courting buyers to bail him out, an executive seeing his wealth of goodwill actually went to work for my client. Together they found new partners and new bankers. Today, he and his partners are doing even bigger and better things.

As another example, the simple act of keeping your word has the unintended consequence of maximizing your credit worthiness and encouraging people to support your endeavors. During the summer of 1993, on a break from her college classes, Sydney took a job at a golf course. Later that summer, her job schedule came into conflict with a family reunion her father had planned. A wealthy businessman, he could not understand why Sydney would not simply quit her job to attend the reunion. Sydney felt that it was important to keep her word to her employer—however irrelevant a summer job at a golf course would ultimately be in the scheme of her life. At the end of that summer, her employer wrote her a glowing letter of recommendation that Sydney used four years later to get her first job at a law firm after graduating from law school.

Let's consider a personal story of mine. In the seventies, my original business partner, Mary, and I were in distress, so we hired an organizational development company to help us. We wanted to be intentional and focused, so we took this positive step to hire this organization to get us back on track. These specialists, who were psychologists for businesses, saw themselves as educators, so they helped me learn how to manage by finding clarity and assigning the appropriate solutions. They started helping me uncover how to intelligently make decisions for the health of the business.

In the process of accessing our strengths, I realized Mary and I were good executors. Once we got a client, we knew how to take care of her. Mary's successor, Greg, her stepson, fit nicely into that mold. We prided ourselves on taking care of the clients we had, but we lacked the skills to do much else but wait for clients to call us. I prided myself on creating an infrastructure in which we put out a superior looking product at a fair price, and so did Greg.

I was worried that our approach to soliciting new business was not up to par. But Jake Jacobs, a superstar accountant who had just left a big accounting firm, was looking for a new firm. At the same time, we were looking for someone who could solicit business. Jake immediately saw the potential in that our infrastructure was such that he could bring in a ton of business and feel secure that we would take care of his clients.

In 1991, Jake started. His job was to secure the clients, and we intended that he would surpass my book of business in four or five years. At the time, we were grossing $1,200,000.

Now, we gross $10,000,000 and we are extremely profitable. But it cannot all be credited directly to business Jake brought to the firm. Though he far exceeded our expectations, his competitive style turned on our competitive juices. Not only did he book a lot of business, but Jake also motivated and coached me to do the same. That first year of Jake's partnership at the firm, I brought in an unprecedented amount of business. The strategic byproduct of my focused decision to align with an expert is that I increased my business-getting success.

For sixteen years, I kept Jake from surpassing me, not because he wasn't doing his job, but because I had a head start, and he encouraged me to keep on running. This is not what I intended, but Jake inspired us all to do more.

Those who do not plan do not come away with these kinds of results. They are always fighting a defensive fight, trying to get out of the way of the elephant rather than looking at the positive outcomes that can come from saying *hello* to the elephant and reaching clarity.

Oh, and by the way, if I had not been taught by that first consultant, Brad Spencer, PhD, new ways to manage, this book would not be sitting on your lap, at your desk, or relaxing with you on the beach! I trust my strategic byproduct was worth the time you spent reading this book.

Choosing the right
trusted advisory team.

THROUGHOUT MY CAREER, my firm has hired trusted advisors to assist us in our efforts. Why, you ask, does a management consultant hire a management consultant?

I think it was Supreme Court Justice Learned Hand who said, "An attorney that represents himself has a fool for a client."

He is right! Of course, some of your decisions can be made without help, but when it comes to complex business, tax, legal, or financial affairs, a knowledgeable, trustworthy consultant or set of consultants can be invaluable in helping you understand what you want and how to get it.

Regardless of your skills, one thing is certain: you are too close to the situation to pull back and objectively evaluate your whole picture. Finding the right team will assist you in defining your clarity and the solutions. If your plans are complex, your advisory team will be more qualified than you to implement the solutions.

In this book, we focus on trusted advisors in business fields, such as accountants, attorneys, investment advisors, life insurance agents, and casualty insurance agents, but a trusted advisor might also be involved in your personal life, such as a clergyman, psychologist, nutritionist, or fitness trainer.

We all want to be surrounded by trustworthy right-hand men or women with whom we feel comfortable over the long haul. Trouble is, trustworthy and loyal do not always add up to competent and reliable, and in many cases, you have to accept that your advisor's reason for being in the relationship is more self-serving than noble.

Of course, the ideal advisor is at once trustworthy, competent, reliable and team-oriented, but those commodities are rare in the real world. In this section, we will take a closer look at different approaches to hiring an advisor and come to a better understanding of when to hire someone with whom you are intimate and when the right choice scores higher on the competence and reliability chart.

Truth is, every person deserves to have at least one trusted advisor, and more can be even better. And when considering your solution, it is critical to have the right team in place.

When deciding mega-important, long lasting, sometimes irrevocable decisions that impact not only you but also the people closest to you,[11] you need a person you can trust without a single nagging doubt—a respected team member you confide in and that you know for certain is reliable and knowledgeable. You want a true professional with the best interest of you, your family, and your business in mind—a person you can trust like your own mother.

GRADING THE ADVISOR

Trust is difficult to define. What components really add up to complete trust? We'll talk about four:

1. Competency,
2. Reliability,
3. Intimacy, and
4. Self-orientation.

Are you able to trust a person because of **competency**? If an advisor knows his stuff, the advisor's experience and background are more likely to lead you to your goals. That person's competency is easy to see and easy to believe, therefore you can let yourself trust.

---

11 Like what kind of sausage to make.

Does trust come from how easily you can **rely** on this person? He does what he says. This person follows through, is timely, courteous, respectful, and shows professionalism in all matters and situations. This advisor is accountable and serious about commitments.

Or is trust something more personal? Is it more linked to the level of openness and **intimacy** you can share with this chosen person? How honest can you really be? Can you divulge your inner thoughts, wishes and wants without feeling judged by this advisor? Do you trust the advisor enough to be completely open, no holds barred? Do you trust the advisor's discretion?

Finally, does trust revolve around the level of **self-orientation** your advisor exhibits? Are you comfortable with the interest he shows on your behalf? Granted, your advisor's job and chosen career is to protect your interests, and you pay him to do so. But if you feel the scale is tipped in his favor, trust is difficult to come by. You want an advisor who is not just looking for the payout, but who is also sincerely concerned about your overall wellbeing.

Trust comes in many shapes and forms. Fortunately, David Maister, Charles Green, and Robert Galford, authors of *The Trusted Advisor* (Free Press, 2000), designed a formula to help evaluate and rate a trusted advisor. The Trusted Advisor Formula pulls together the most important components that go into a long-term, sustainable relationship with a trusted advisor, and the formula creates a rating system that can help you decide if the advisor is right for you.

Obviously, what is most valuable to some is not to others. The formula allows for these variances. Based on a one-to-ten scale, a trusted advisor's score is based on the following formula:

$$\frac{C+R+I}{S} = TA$$

The sum of Competence + Reliability + Intimacy
divided by Self-Orientation
Equals
A number that rates the likelihood that a
particular advisor is truly a trusted advisor

The higher the number, with thirty being the most trusted and 0.3 being the least trusted, the more intensely you will trust your advisor. You could have a number of trusted advisors, but a trusted advisor who earns a three is not as trusted as an advisor who earns a nine.

C = Competence[12]

Competence is the level of expertise and knowledge you believe your advisor has. Competence is not necessarily gauged by the years of experience he has, but instead by the quality of experience. His competence elicits your confidence. A competent advisor makes you feel that you are in capable hands.

R = Reliability

Reliability means that you do not question your advisor's word. You know that he will follow through and walk the walk. He says what he means and he means what he says. Appointments are kept, paperwork is complete, research is thorough, and the information you get is accurate.

I = Intimacy

Intimacy is all about the relationship you share with this person. Can you be completely open or are you somewhat guarded? If you find yourself holding back, you are not going to be satisfied with the end results of your decision-making or plan. If you feel that you can divulge unabashedly, you have a high level of intimacy with this person. If you are concerned with revealing certain aspects of your personal business, this will be a lower rating on the intimacy scale.

Can you see yourself being intimate with this person? This is a gut feeling. Do you connect? Can you see that the advisor has empathy in the way he reacts to your comments and feelings?

---

12 Maister, Green, and Galford use "credibility" instead of "competence." Truth be told, the two terms have much overlap, but I prefer competence and have, with the permission of the authors, taken the liberty to substitute terms.

S = Self-Orientation

Self-orientation in this formula is defined as the level of self-interest your trusted advisor exhibits. Unlike the other three components, a low rating is positive, indicating that the advisor is more in it for you than himself. A high number means it's all about numero uno: him.

Obviously, all advisors have a certain level of self-interest—they are exchanging services for income. But when considering the quality of interest the advisor has in you, self-orientation indicates whether the advisor cares about delivering honest value. Is he going through the motions because he wants the paycheck, or is he genuinely invested in your success?

EVALUATING THE ADVISOR

Ideally, all your advisors will rank well in each category. Realistically, however, you will be surrounded by some team members who are competent and reliable but highly self-oriented, as well as others who have your back but are not entirely skilled.

The key is filling the right advisors in the right spots. When it comes to creating a team of advisors, you want to consider Fithian's Planning Horizon™ and assign intimate, selfless advisors to the "above-the-line" quadrants and reliable, competent advisors to the "below-the-line" quadrants.

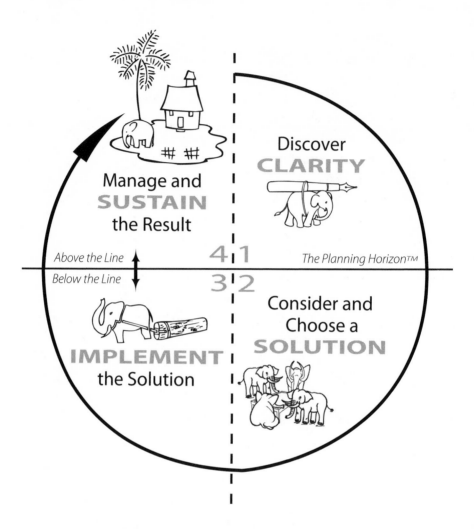

The Planning Horizon™ concept, developed and improved by the late Scott Fithian and his brother Todd, was first presented in Scott's book, **Value-Based Estate Planning**.

An intimate and selfless advisor is more likely to have your best interest in mind when creating clarity and sustainability (Quadrants One and Four), but when it comes time to craft and implement solutions (Quadrants Two and Three), you need competent, reliable advisors.

Let's work through some common examples.

COLLEGE BUDDY

Your college fraternity brother, with whom you spent some intimately fun time, graduated with an M.B.A. and went to work for Big Time Lawyer & Son. You know he is sufficiently adequate in his work, has some practical knowledge, and features a solid list of clients. However, he has never been promoted to a higher level and still likes to bend his elbow at the neighborhood bar. A very likable guy, he gets along great with people and still holds some secrets of college life that you would rather have remain in both of your memory files.

It is safe to say that you can rate College Buddy high on the **Intimacy** realm. Let's assign him a **10**. But as far as **Competence** he'd rank right around a **3**. **Reliability** may be a little higher, but still questionable, so let's give him a **4**.

He is one of your best buddies, so you know that he has your best interest in mind. For **Self–Orientation** he rates a **2**. (Remember the lower the number, the lower his self-interest.)

When you plug in the numbers, College Buddy looks like this:

$$\frac{3+4+10}{2} = 8.5$$

His score is an **8.5**, an impressive number, depending on your focus. His intimacy and self-orientation scores reflect that College Buddy may be the right choice for above-the-line activities, such as vision discovery (Quadrant One) and annual reviews to make sure your goals haven't changed (Quadrant Four). You will also most likely have clarity in that you know where he is coming from, his shortcomings and all. This advisor will get you through some basic planning and will have your financial interests first in mind.

But what's lacking with this person comes from Quadrants Two and Three (reliability and competence). You won't get creative and cutting-edge solutions followed by precision implementation.

His poor scores in reliability and competency do not mean College Buddy is the wrong advisor; they mean College Buddy should not be relied upon when you are in the Solutions and Implementation Quadrants.

Let's try a contrasting example.

SMARTY PANTS

Smarty Pants graduated with a double degree in finance and international business from Harvard. You knew of her, but you do not run in the same circles. A serious person who owns her own financial advising company, she knows her numbers.

Smarty Pants is considered somewhat aloof and cool in her professional dealings as well as social settings. She spends late nights at the office and doesn't have much time for a personal life. Her professional approach is intense. She has one way to address any problem: research and model every possible permutation. She bills every minute and seems to be unaware of the balance between careful research and value. In other words, she doesn't have a perspective.

No question, Smarty Pants will rank high in **Competence** and **Reliability** (**9** and **8**). As for **Intimacy**, it's just a little too hard to warm up to her so she scores a **4**. **Self-Orientation** is going to be high number. After all she has a business to run with high overhead and several employees to pay. Let's assign her a **7**.

Put all her numbers together and it looks like this:

$$\frac{9+8+4}{7} = 3$$

Smarty Pants scores a **3**. A low number in isolation, but upon closer look, a high value if you are looking for solutions and implementation strategies.

Let's take a look at our third example.

YOUNG & ENERGETIC

You know the type, though they have become increasingly rare in an age where youth seems to view a job as an entitlement. This recent college graduate is a throwback. He will do whatever you ask, whether checking the market report or getting you coffee. All references from the school and first employer effusively praise his work ethic, intelligence, and bright future. You like his spark.

His eagerness to please ensures persistence and dedication, earning a high rating in the **Reliability** category, as high as a **9**. His youth might mean an age gap that limits **Intimacy**, but the desire to please and learn will likely offset this difference, making this area a solid **6**. As for **Competency**, you will have to rely on your instincts. Everything points to him being smart and capable, but he is cutting his teeth. It's tough to give Young & Energetic more than a **5** for **Competency**. This brings us to **Self-Orientation**, another difficult area to gauge. Like all people his age, Young & Energetic wants to improve his lot, but the desire to grow and please demands a selflessness that assigns him the number **4**.

Here's how Young & Energetic looks:

$$\frac{5+9+6}{4} = 5$$

The result: **5**.

Your gut might tell you this trusted advisor is for you. Compared to the college chum, this advisor's rating is low. But College Buddy has reached his summit, and Young & Energetic is still rising to the top. What you might sacrifice in the **Competency** realm in the short term might pay off with long-term dividends in **Reliability** and **Self-Orientation**. Over time, your faith in this person may lead to a greater mutual appreciation and openness to share on your part. This will ultimately increase the **Intimacy** number. Furthermore, the one area of early concern—**Competency**—can be taught to a reliable, loyal, self-starter who sees that your best interests are also his.

PUTTING IT ALL TOGETHER

It's difficult to find one trusted advisor when so much is on the line. The Trusted Advisor Formula simplifies and clarifies the advantages or disadvantages someone brings to your table. What's most important to keep in mind while you're assessing an advisor is that your focus matches your specific needs.

Let's review the four quadrants.

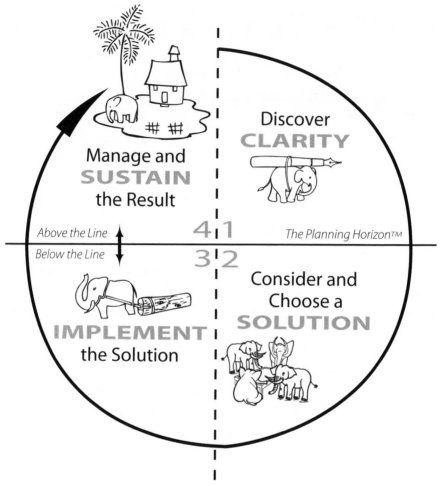

Quadrants One and Four (clarity and sustainability), the vision-setting and planning foundation of goal-setting, are "above-the-line" needs, and require a different kind of planning than necessary for Quadrants Two and Three (implementation, solutions), the "below-the-line" quadrants. So though College Buddy scores higher than Smarty Pants overall, you certainly would not want to trust your solution and implementation to College Buddy.[13]

---

[13] Maybe if you get College Buddy and Smarty Pants together, their child will be the perfect all-around advisor.

ABOVE-THE-LINE ADVISORS

As we discussed in earlier chapters, you need to have clarity of your personal situation, goals, and desired outcome. Later, you will learn that you must constantly review this through a sustainability plan. This type of vision-setting requires advisors who scores high in intimacy and low in self-orientation. You have to be able to discuss delicate matters and personal wishes and trust that it won't come back to bite you. They need to shine in the clarity planning process because clarity can be difficult to get to. Great tax planners can be great clarity planners, but great clarity planners need not be great tax planners. They must be committed to you, and you must feel free to disclose personal information.

BELOW-THE-LINE ADVISORS

Now, let's say that you are already clear on your goals and have clarity in what basic solutions are available to you. Let's also say that you have some sticky situations perhaps involving family members, second marriages, property, assets, an inheritance, or trust fund. Suffice it to say, you are more in need of solutions and implementing, the "below-the-line" needs.

If these areas are your focus, your trusted advisor needs to score higher in the reliability and competency realms. You also need an advisor who is strong on implementation and does what he says he's going to do. He's thorough and nothing falls between the cracks. He gets the job done the way you want, and it matters not whether he has your long-term interests at heart, or whether you feel intimate with him. For these short-term, immediate-fix goals, you need someone to file the papers, design the solutions, and move on. Job done.

The point is that it's critical to have the right trusted advisor or team of advisors working for you. For the crucial matters in your life, the right person or team makes all the difference. You may end up with undesirable results if you're listening and following the wrong person's advice. Just because he's a likable fellow, and someone you've known for a long time, doesn't mean College Buddy provides you with the best counsel.

If you think of competence and reliability as a commodity, you may think that they are easy to acquire. To be sure, competent professionals

are a dime a dozen and readily available. You can use Google to find them. Less common, though, are reliable advisors. A lot of people know their stuff (are competent), but even fewer have their marbles together and processes in place so they can maintain quality work in volume. And intimacy and low self-orientation are even harder to find; they are also less tangible. You cannot be intimate with just anyone. Close relationships never come easily. They require a more soulful connection and more of a time commitment. If you're looking for someone to walk you through clarity of vision, this person must be a confidant. In the end, intimate relationships are worth the output, no matter the outcome. Nothing ventured, nothing gained.

High self-orientation, as we said previously, is not always a bad thing. However, if your perception is that this guy is just grinding the fees, you won't be open to hearing what he has to say. You'll have a mental block of counting coins, which means he won't work for clarity or sustainability. If you were in an investment situation that can make or save you some serious dollars, you actually would prefer an advisor who scores high in self-orientation in solutions and implementation. He knows the more money you make (or save), the higher his paycheck or return will be.

If all of this sounds like too much to put on one person, you're probably right. What most clients need is a cadre of trusted counselors. This should be a team with a clear picture of your vision, mission, and goals. But, even more important, they can competently execute below-the-line strategies, tactics, and tools.

We often find that our clients' previous experience leads them to go with a team that meets the basics: vision and mission statements, goal setting, and predictable solutions. Even though they do focus on above-the-line services, they give short attention to these areas. Their pricing structures are based on getting something—anything—done as opposed to getting the right thing done. They fail to offer, properly contextual, below-the-line advice. Their strategies are faulty, ill-timed, or just plain off the mark. It's almost as if some advisors throw solutions against the wall like noodles. Some stick, some don't, but the advisors always get paid.

As the client, you should expect your trusted advisor to call on someone with more expertise in an area in which he does not excel. If your advisor doesn't have the expertise to offer, he should acquiesce to someone smarter or more experienced. A trusted advisor who is confident in his abilities isn't threatened by admitting the need to bring in someone else with more direct knowledge. This is where the team approach enters, and offers a more well rounded and comprehensive service. It is often the best of both worlds.

On the flip side, if you have developed a close, intimate relationship with your trusted advisor, you should be willing to release him to seek guidance from another advisor. Don't let penny-pinching, fear, or lack of trust stand in your way. Giving your advisor permission to seek the resources he needs to give you the best counsel is a win/win situation.

BEING IN CONTROL OF THE PROCESS.

DESPITE THE NEED FOR A TEAM of trusted advisors who sit on your panel, I am a strong proponent of remaining in control of the process. We hear regularly of the musicians, actors, and celebrities who relinquish control of their financial lives to their managers or advisors, only to wake up and discover that their money has been stolen and trust abused.

If you give someone else control of your money, rest assured that they will take control. Though you might rely on many people—an accountant, tax attorney, legacy planner, and estate planning attorney—you must sit at the head of the table and raise your hand when you do not understand something or do not agree.

When acting intentionally, you are the one calling the shots. Think back to my client who for years failed to sign his estate planning documents. My client was failing to implement these plans because he was not making the call, instead relying on an impersonal attorney.

When the Clarity Quadrant is successfully negotiated, you have developed your goals and understand better than ever where you came from. It is your story, your family, your business, and your goals. When you are clear about where you are going, who can be a better conductor of your affairs? This clarity is **very powerful**. No tax, legal, or insurance expert can take that power unless you surrender it. You may not be an expert in those areas, but you are an expert in the most important area: you.

That said, allow your trusted advisor to do his or her job. If you find yourself watching the clock, wishing that your advisor's time is more concise and that he spend less time in discussion and more time in action, you either have the wrong advisory team, or you do not see the connection between your advisor and your overall mission. Your advisor is seeking clarity and can only do so by completely understanding your mission, vision, values, and goals. Watching the clock is not conducive to clarity, nor does it generate creative solutions on the part of the advisor.

While it is appropriate for you to sit at the table and enunciate your goals, you must make sure that your advisors are pulling the wagon in the same direction. To do this, you must fight against your natural desire to run a tight ship, setting aggressive deadlines, and being hard-nosed. Creative solutions are a team effort, and in a professional setting, they result in profit or savings that far exceed their cost. If the trusted advisors are doing their jobs, and you allow them the time, freedom, and ability to be creative, your solutions will be highly desired, creative, and effective.

Managing by Gut.

Many successful businesses not only employ a terrific team of consultants to assist them in finding the right solutions to realize their clarified goals, they also employ specific tools. These might include "360 Degree" evaluations, retreats, diagnostic tools, flash reports, computer programs, personality testing, and the like. This chapter is devoted to just one of these tools, which has promoted clarity in solutions in my business for over a decade.

Back in the nineties, I was having breakfast with a friend in the insurance business, Art. Art told me about an instrument that could tell me how I best liked to work and understand why I felt stress when working with certain people. The instrument would also provide some guidance when I was feeling sapped for energy. The instrument is called the Kolbe A Index.

I finished breakfast with Art and went to my office, immediately went to Kolbe.com, and proceeded to purchase and take the Kolbe A Index online (www.kolbe.com). The moment that I read my result I became a devotee of the Kolbe Wisdom. We use it in our business every day. We hire employees using its methodology. We build work teams with a view toward the information we know because of using it. We became certified to give Kolbe advice and apply it to our clients' problems.

Kathy Kolbe began to develop the Kolbe Wisdom in the mid 1980s. She understood that many instruments measured intellect (IQ) and measured the affective mind (personality tests) but she could not find one that helped explain how people actually go about acting if they are free to be themselves. This is known as the Conative Mind. She noticed and then documented that people are moved to action by gathering facts (Fact Finders), creating patterns or process (Follow Throughs), dealing with the unknown and being intuitive (Quick Starters), or modeling and making tangible their solutions (Implementors).

A family affair, Kolbe Corp has developed evaluative tools that help people understand how they are hard wired and how they will go about solving problems given the freedom to be themselves. Their tools help you understand how you compare yourself to your perception of what others want you to be. Their tools help compare yourself to the expectations that others place on you. So many find themselves in positions that call on them to work in modes that are not their strong suits and, in fact, work against their natural inclinations. Our consultation with clients using the Kolbe Wisdom can suggest ways to alleviate that stress by redefining roles, changing work teams, and encouraging realistic expectations by supervisors.

Most tools try to define what folks are not good at and encourage them to do better. Kolbe tells folks to determine what they are good at and create conditions that can leverage those strengths for what they want to accomplish. The hard wiring that Kolbe helps uncover are the instincts that can make you successful. It describes why your gut tells you to do something or work in a certain way. I encourage all who read this book to take a look at Kolbe. Virtually everyone I know finds it an incredibly useful addition to their arsenal of solutions.

At my firm, the use of Kolbe Wisdom has resulted in reduced turnover, better morale, and a better success rate in hiring. I can't begin to tell you how terrific it has been in helping raise my children!

KEY POINTS

In Quadrant Two, we focus on solutions, defining how we will reach the goals discovered in Quadrant One. Solutions should be SMART (specific, measurable, actionable, relevant, and time-bounded), detailing exactly what actions a goal entails. As well, consider the following when defining a solution.

Obstacles are stepping stones that narrow the solution. Most obstacles actually represent a stepping stone that moves a person closer to a goal. Instead of being deterred by obstacles, incorporate them into your solution by creating a plan to overcome them. By identifying a goal and the obstacles that might block this goal, a person can focus his efforts to identify a solution that will allow him to overcome obstacles.

Sausage is subjective. Your solution must resonate with your tastes. No one solution fits all. Make sure that you can answer the following critical questions before implementing a solution:

- *Do I completely understand the solution that is being proposed?*
- *What is it?*
- *How is it applicable?*
- *How does it work?*
- *What can go wrong?*
- *Who must be involved?*
- *How much does it cost to implement?*
- *How much does it cost to sustain?*
- *What must be done to sustain it?*

The Artichoke Theory. Conquer obstacles and implement solutions the same way you eat an artichoke: one leaf at a time. Keep things simple by breaking them into small, achievable steps, and keep all steps under the umbrella of the main goal.

Slow down. You are in a hurry. When faced with implementing an important goal, slow down. Because you are in a hurry, take deep breaths and remind yourself to get un-nervous. Only then will you have the wherewithal to address obstacles, make rational decisions, and move your plans forward.

The Law of Unintended Consequences. All conduct has unintended consequences. The unintended consequences of negative or unfocused behavior are inevitably negative. Positive conduct, on the other hand, is inevitably rewarded with unintended positive consequences (which we call "strategic byproducts). Strategic byproducts of positive or focused behavior are always positive because the intentionality of planning, the purposefulness of goals, and the alignment of goals with values all create a solid base with which other positive things can attach.

Choosing the right trusted advisory team. Supreme Court Justice Learned Hand said, "An attorney that represents himself has a fool for a client!" When it comes to complex and critical goals, a knowledgeable team is invaluable. Use the Trusted Advisor Formula to measure competence, reliability, intimacy, and self-orientation, creating a team of advisors who can handle both "above-the-line" activities (clarity and sustainability) and "below-the-line" activities (solutions and implementation).

Being in control of the process. No one should be clearer about your goals than you. Though you might rely on many people—an accountant, a tax attorney, a legacy planner, or an estate planning attorney—you must sit at the head of the table and raise your hand when you do not understand or agree with something.

Managing by gut. The Kolbe A Index (www.kolbe.com) is an instrument that measures a person's hard wiring. If left to his own devices, how will a person go about acting? Integrated into a strategic plan, Kolbe's tools help a business or person assess proper team roles, set realistic expectations, and evaluate expectations.

See the Quadrant Thinking Conductor for a step-by-step process to develop solutions.

IMPLEMENTATION

Quadrant Three | IMPLEMENTATION

AT SOME POINT IN ANY VENTURE, the time comes to stop planning and start acting. This transition moves you into the Implementation Quadrant, and it occurs when you can answer the following critical questions with confidence:

1. *What does the ideal outcome look like?*
2. *What is the solution?*
3. *How is it applicable to the overall vision and goals?*
4. *What are the steps necessary to make it work?*
5. *What can go wrong?*
6. *Who are the trusted advisors that must be involved?*
7. *Who else must be involved?*
8. *How much does it cost to implement?*
9. *How much does it cost to sustain?*
10. *What must be done to sustain it?*

When done properly, working through the Clarity and Solution Quadrants will lead you to the answers to these questions and marks the time for you to put your solution into action.

So why are you reading this? Go forth and implement!

JUST KIDDING!

IN A CERTAIN WAY, QUADRANT THREE is the easiest of the quadrants, but it can also be the trickiest. On one hand, if you have achieved clarity and confidently identified an effective solution, the bulk of the hard work is done. On the other hand, implementation presents a barrier in that many people crave the safety of perpetual planning. Once you implement a plan, you will have outcomes whereby you (and others) can judge your success. This can be scary.[1]

In addition to stasis, implementation also requires you to work against procrastination and buyer's remorse.

In this section, you will learn how to overcome these barriers to success, as well as many tricks and tools to implementing your solutions.

---

[1] Scary like Freddy Krueger or pineapple on pizza (although I, for one, really like pineapple on pizza).

PUSHING AGAINST GRAVITY.

MANY YEARS HAVE PASSED since I first walked through the doors of Ulysses S. Grant High School, but I remember it with vivid detail. As much as I wanted to grow up and enter the elite world of the upperclassmen, I also longed for the safety and comfort of Millikin[2] Junior High School. Since then, that odd coupling of fear and anticipation has replicated itself many times over: the first time I drove a car; the first time I started a new job. It happened again recently when I decided to start exercising. I felt out of place, like the hard-bodied gym-goers were making fun of my light dumbbells and heavy breathing. I knew I wanted change, but I craved comfort food and a warm couch.

Change *per se* is difficult. Breaking out of our habits and routines deprives us of the safety of the familiar and puts us on a path that can be uncomfortable and even scary. It takes willpower to put yourself in a new situation. It is far easier to sit back in your recliner and watch the sports channel while drinking a beer and munching potato chips.[3] But success requires breaking out of our comfort zones, changing patterns, and breaking routines.

Aggravating matters, anytime you try something new, the world's forces try to keep you within the sphere you are in, throwing obstacles at you that—like gravity—push you into place.

The question is: Do you back off (return to the status quo), or do you push back (evaluate the obstacles and create a plan to move past them)?

And if you want to push back, how will you escape from stasis?

---

2 And cookies.
3 Maybe even undo the top button on your pants.

The first tool is to make the transition **part** of your solution. By incorporating a plan to transition into action, we can overcome the barrier of stasis and push against gravity.

If my goal is to lose fifteen pounds in three months, my solution should say when those three months start, and what the very first action is that I must take toward my goal. And that first step should be small. Because walking into a gym will likely intimidate me, I can make my first step something simple like taking a thirty-minute brisk walk with my wife each evening for two weeks in preparation for my first trip to the gym.

Some plans require an easy transition. For me, jumping head over heels into a new diet and exercise regimen is a recipe for disaster. My eventual success depends on my ability to wean myself off high carbohydrate junk foods. Telling me that I must start eating nothing but fruit, vegetables, fish, and chicken causes me great panic. I have tried this before, and it has not worked. But if I slowly change my behavior, I will gradually adopt new habits and become a healthier person. The implementation portion of my solution, therefore, might include something like this:

1. **Weeks One and Two:** Thirty-minute brisk walks with my wife each evening beginning March 1. Replace lattés with black coffee.

2. **Weeks Two through Six:** Continue Weeks One and Two behavior. Drink eight glasses of water daily. Spend thirty minutes in the gym three times a week.

3. **Weeks Seven through Ten:** Continue Weeks One through Six behavior. Nightly, make next day's meal plan, to consist of five small meals instead of three large meals and snacks throughout.

4. **Week Eleven:** Continue Weeks One through Ten behavior. Consult with a nutritionist to change my eating habits.

5. **Week Twelve and ongoing:** Continue nightly walks, gym schedule, and implement nutritionist's plan. Schedule quarterly meetings with a nutritionist to monitor my progress.

With this plan, I can eat the elephant one bite at a time, while implementing all components of the solution would surely be a disaster. Most likely, I would start cheating on Day Two during my mid-afternoon crash of energy. After sneaking to the vending machine, I would call the entire solution a failure and neglect to implement even the simple components such as nightly walks with my wife and drinking black coffee instead of lattés.

Let's consider a business example. Assume that you have an expanding enterprise and you want to relocate your business from your garage to a high-rise office structure that would be closer to your clientele. Instead of hurrying out and signing a long-term lease, you might want to start by simply visiting office buildings and just sitting there during the busiest times of the day. Who comes in and goes out? Do they look happy or sad? How are they dressed? Before signing the lease, you might have lunch at the local eateries to see whether the environment feels comfortable. If it feels good, you can engage a leasing agent to negotiate for you. Finally, you might want to obligate to a very limited-time lease or sublease so that you can understand what it is you like and dislike about your space before you make a long-term commitment.

That said, the reset button is often more effective than a gradual transition. Some solutions require an implementation that is a clean and clear break from the old ways of doing things (or not doing them) and the new way. If I plan to implement a new business plan, I might take my employees on a retreat, which will mark the end of the old way of doing business. In this scenario, trying to change gradually is likely not effective as employees would not feel a sense of urgency. Instead, they would simply maintain the status quo, pushing changes to the backburner.

Knowing when to choose between a gradual change and a mega-change is a critical part of implementation. Sometimes, you will simply know intuitively which to choose, but having a process that helps you decide will not hurt. Ask yourself the following questions:

- *Is it easier for me to get excited about something if I know I get to give it 100 percent?* You might be an all-or-nothing person who thrives on pulling the trigger.

- *Do the individual steps necessary to bring this project up to speed seem overwhelming?* If so, a gradual change might be more effective.

- *Can all the steps necessary to bring this project up to speed be done at once, or does one step have a prerequisite?* If the latter is true, a gradual change is necessary.

- *How many opportunities will I have to revisit implementation?* You should consider changing everything at once if the solution requires implementation immediately or if you are only going to have one chance for a successful implementation. For instance, if you are implementing a new business plan and have a four-day retreat scheduled with your staff, this may represent the only opportunity for training, in which case full implementation should happen immediately so that it remains fresh in your employees' minds.

- *Once implemented, have I taken irrevocable steps that will materially change the status quo?* If not, you might consider making your steps larger and more meaningful.

Pushing against gravity also requires that your actions fall under the umbrella of your overarching mission, vision, or goal. If implementation seems to be a hassle, it may be that your solution does not fall under the purview of your commander's intent, a phrase I borrow from the military that was described by Chip and Dan Heath, authors of *Made to Stick*. Think of the commander's intent as your overarching goal—the umbrella defining your action. You identified your commander's intent during the Clarity Quadrant. It is the one thing or set of things, above all else, that you want to get accomplished. When things are out of control or extremely hectic, the commander's intent keeps you focused on the **one thing** that you need to do. If your solution is not relevant to the commander's intent, you will likely be uninspired to implement it.

On the other hand, if you have an emotionally compelling vision that is directly tied to your solution, your resolve to implement the solution will remain strong even if the plan is physically and emotionally draining.

Consider, Tim Borland. In 2007, this thirty-one-year-old runner decided to help raise awareness of a rare degenerative children's disease known as A-T.[4] Borland thought that he could best generate media attention, and thereby promote the public's awareness, if he set a goal so outrageous it could not be ignored. His mission: run sixty-three marathons in sixty-three days. Planning it was both mentally and physically simple. He created a training schedule and found sixty-three marathons on sixty-three consecutive days.

The plan's implementation, however, was not simple. The first few weeks were tough on Borland, and by the midway point, I imagine he was questioning his resolve, thinking, *This is a lot harder than I thought it would be.*

If Borland was simply running sixty-three marathons in sixty-three days for the heck of it, he might have been tempted to quit on those days when he felt doubt. But because his plan was tied to an emotionally compelling vision of increasing awareness for A-T, Borland completed all sixty-three marathons on November 4, 2007. He also ran most of them while pushing a jogging stroller occupied by a child with A-T. Newspaper and media outlets across the country, including *USA Today* and National Public Radio, took notice.

A first-century Zen master said, "When walking, just walk. When sitting, just sit. Above all, don't wobble." Or, when running sixty-three marathons in sixty-three days, just run sixty-three marathons in sixty-three days. If your plan ties into the commander's intent, you can push your doubts aside and put one foot in front of the other.

---

4 Ataxia-telangiectasia combines the symptoms of cerebral palsy, muscular dystrophy, cystic fibrosis, and cancer.

Just do it.

THE RULES OF IMPLEMENTATION boil down to one basic rule: just do it.

Procrastination is the strongest force that can stop us from successfully implementing our solution. Procrastination can have many sources, but a common one is the feeling of being overwhelmed. How many times have we faced a pile of work only to find that it is impossible for us to start?

Procrastination is a self-protective mechanism: we feel that we cannot accomplish some goal, so we do not start.

| QUESTION |
How do we fight procrastination?[5]

| ANSWER |
Identify some small part of the overall task that we can do.

For instance, I recently spoke with Susie, a long-time client. A successful business owner, Susie could not face completing her estate planning. Her estate was sizeable with an armamentarium[6] of moving parts. Unless she completed her estate plan, Susie could die without a will: not at all the ideal situation. She was ignoring her elephant because she did not understand the concept of eating the elephant one bite at a time.

---

5 Resist the temptation to check your e-mail.
6 Don't you just love those big words! If you don't know what this means just wait for my next book titled *Using Big Words You Can't Define for Fun and Profit.*

I suggested that Susie approach the estate planning process one step at a time. She could start with a basic plan that would protect her assets and deliver simple distributions to her beneficiaries. Because complications deterred Susie, she should not seek to make it the most effective or the most sophisticated plan. The plan did not need to be perfect; it needed to be good enough. The point was not to make a perfect plan. Some plan was better than no plan. Some plan would make her untimely death significantly easier for those she left behind. Some plan would stop some amount of estate taxation. Some plan would take a small step toward passing her values along to her loved ones.

With this small step out of the way, Susie can take the next step: modifying the plan so that it becomes a little stronger. In six months, she can review it again, and again six months later.[7]

In most cases, taking one small action will catapult you past procrastination into action. But sometimes more steps are required. The important part is to identify the most pressing action you can take, and then to take it immediately, working through it until it is complete, ignoring the steps that will have to follow it.

---

[7] Elephant bites are kind of like Lay's potato chips: betcha can't eat just one!

Using a process.

I AM ATTRACTED TO PROCESSES in a way that should make my wife jealous. The idea that a process exists that will move me from Point A to Point B is exciting. Processes whisper promises into my ear: "If you do X, Y will happen."

Of course, nothing in life is a guarantee. The "couldn't-have-knowns" wreak havoc on plans so that even the best-planned process can, from time to time, be rendered useless. But failing to use a process because something unexpected **could** happen is simply foolish. This concept is critical throughout Quadrant Thinking. At its core, Quadrant Thinking is a process that moves a person from Point A to Point B to Point C to Point D.

At Point C—Quadrant Three: Implementation—I am driven to remind you that Quadrant Thinking requires that you use a formal and **written** process if you are implementing complex solutions. Even something as seemingly simple as losing fifteen pounds or scheduling time for a vacation is more likely to come to fruition if you use a formal plan that moves you from one point (the current) to the next (the ideal goal).

A successful implementation requires that you take control as much as possible. You must identify and make a plan to control for all the knowns so that the unknowns are less of an issue. Too many goals fall to the wayside during the Implementation Quadrant because their owners did not create a formal plan that prepares and outlines the steps necessary to move from one point to another point. They simply hold a goal loosely, hoping that it will someday come true without any plan to make it happen.[8]

---

8 Like cleaning out the garage.

These people argue that plans are useless because of the many variables in life. They cannot possibly know where tomorrow will take them. Yet I stand armored, ready to defend the honor of processes.[9]

If you believe that there are too many arbitrary variables to make a successful plan, you have given up. And in doing so, you have planned for something: you have planned to fail. You have raised the white flag and surrendered your goals. It is akin to saying, "I might not be able to achieve my goal; therefore I cannot achieve my goal."

We all know this is pure rubbish, right?

You might also think that all this Quadrant Thinking is common sense. *Why write it out when it seems so simple. It's easy: set a goal and then just do it.* You might be correct about one thing: Quadrant Thinking **is** simple, but it isn't easy. If it were, more people would have clarity and be on the path to achieving their dreams.

The most successful, accomplished individuals will all attest to the power of crafting a written plan. Writing your plan helps you achieve your goals. Some argue providence—simply by writing your goals, you will cause the universe to work in your favor, setting into motion a stream of events that will lead to the eventual realization of your written goal. Others argue that the act of writing a blueprint simultaneously creates a neural pathway, bushwhacking the way for your goal to reach fruition.

This is a little too California-hippie for some people, and the more realistic explanation of the connection between written goals and their eventual success is that written goals require specificity. By committing to a plan in writing, you begin asking yourself all sorts of questions as to how your plan will work. These answers, then, become the tools you need when it comes time to implement your plan.

One might wonder: *If I, a no-process person, needs only a skeleton of a process, why is a written process necessary?* The answer is that writing helps one consider **all** the elements that might be necessary to successfully imple-

---

9 My friend Kathy Kolbe has convinced me that a portion of the population can be effective without much in the way of a formal process. I believe that, but even for them, some modicum of process **must** be used to accomplish most complex planning. The differentiation is a matter of degree and intensity. Some folks need a skeleton of a process and some need a step-by-step process.

ment your solution. It can be written on the back of a napkin, but it must be written. At the end of this book, you will find the Quadrant Thinking Conductor. This tool outlines the generic process, serving as the foundation for your written plan. By building upon the Conductor and altering it to apply to your specific plan, obstacle, or elephant, your transition from solutions to implementation will be clearly thought out and documented.

CREATING ACCOUNTABILITY.

ONE OF THE PERKS OF MY POSITION is that few folks are my superiors. I understand that my job is to serve my clients, and more often than not, my cat is in charge of my home, but when it comes down to it, I'm my own boss. I worked hard for years to get here. You would think I would be more grateful. But instead, I'm constantly looking for people to hold me accountable.

I know that any solution I try to implement will not be successful unless I feel accountable to someone or something.

I do have two of my partners, Greg and Jake, but they are my equals in business. Before Greg and Jake, there was Mary, Greg's stepmother. Back then, I felt accountable to Mary. She was my senior accountant so, although we were partners, we still had a mentor/mentee relationship. So long as Mary was in the mix, I felt incredibly accountable.

Mary retired in the mid 1980s and, as I alluded to earlier, things began to stagnate. Greg and I were, and still are, great buddies. We worked and played hard. Things weren't bad but they never progressed. We simply did not hold each other accountable for any behavior. We made sure we kept our promises to our clients, but we did little to grow our business. Greg and I had camaraderie. We were equals, and we worried that creating a system where one was accountable to another would upset the balance.

By 1990 we woke up. We realized that we were missing important ingredients from a business perspective. Our first thought was that we needed to emphasize sales and marketing, so we associated good ol' Jake to fill in the holes. Jake energized our marketing, started bringing in tons of clients, and motivated us to bring clients in ourselves.

Another strategic byproduct of partnering with Jake was that we suddenly felt accountable for our actions. We liked Jake, but our relationship with Jake was business. We treated him with the same respect we treated our clients. We knew that we had promised Jake certain things that would require us to act responsibly, so we did. Over time, we realized that Jake's presence forced us into action, so when he became more of a friend than a business colleague, we turned to coaches and advisors to make sure we would move the business forward.

When expected to meet certain criteria, most people will work toward these standards.[10] This is why people who are accountable are much more likely to achieve their goals. Liken this to a child who is given boundaries and consequences for his actions. A child who has no boundaries will continue sticking peas in his nostrils for years to come, which will be embarrassing when he turns thirty.

The problem with success is that the higher we climb on the corporate ladder, the fewer people there are to hold us accountable. When this happens, we must intentionally create artificial accountability.

Accountability comes in several forms: it can be a promise to someone who will hold you accountable. Accountability can be a declaration to your company of your goals. Accountability might even be as simple as creating a rewards system whereby you will treat yourself or your company to something fun upon meeting goals.

The key to successfully creating accountability is to make sure that the stakes are large. If you create an aggressive plan that sets high sales goals for your team, offering no incentives or consequences for the final result, and then never follow up, how successful do you think your team will be in implementing the plan? On the other hand, if you promise to reward your team with a large bonus check if they meet their goals, your team will jump right into action.

When no natural form of accountability exists, you can voluntarily decide to publish your solution to family, friends, or business associates along with your anticipated results, and then set a date whereby you will either deliver the promised results, or pay an imposed consequence.

---

10 Unless they are losers.

Consider this: if you set a goal of increasing your sales record by 10 percent and then promise your business partners that you will pay them each $10,000 if you fail to hit your mark, do you think you will implement the plan? You betcha! If the stakes are high enough, you will take action.

Combating buyer's remorse.

Hal and Jim are brothers-in-law. They purchased their Tucson-based business, Two Sons Distributors, from Jim's father (Hal's father-in-law). The business had two radically different divisions: Jim's division supplied parts to the aerospace industry; the other distributed plumbing supplies and was headed by Hal.

As the aerospace industry in Arizona and its neighbor, Southern California, shrank in size, Jim found himself increasingly frantic about the little growth and lesser profits. Hal, on the other hand, was less frantic because the plumbing side of the business was growing each year. Hal had successfully developed a distribution model that encouraged growth in multiple geographical markets.

Both Hal and Jim thought that the aerospace division should wind down and the plumbing division should occupy the entirety of the brothers-in-laws' efforts.

Feeling marginalized, Jim came to me to discuss the possibility of selling his share of the business. We collectively decided to embark on a clarity project. Jim, Hal, and I met to begin Quadrant One planning. In our discussions, Hal said that he too would be interested in selling the business if the right price could be obtained. We identified "the right price," a number both Hal and Jim agreed upon, and we then moved into Quadrant Two: Solutions.

While doing our due diligence in the solutions phase, we met with several investment banks that could evaluate how realistic the desired sell-out price was. We learned that "the right price" was realistic, and then some. After searching for a trusted investment banker to serve on the advisory team, we drew contracts and laid plans to chart a course for the company that would build its value and set the stage for a sale in the next eighteen months.

It was now time for Quadrant Three: Implementation. We called Hal to sign contracts and start the processes that would maximize the sales values of the company. But Hal failed to make these moves.

Not only was Hal failing to implement, but he was also moving full steam ahead with plans to expand the plumbing distribution business. The plan would reduce earnings in the near-term and devalue the business. Though the five-year profits were promising, he was hardly embarking on behavior that indicated a move toward increasing value and selling the business.

I immediately knew what was happening. Hal had buyer's remorse. Or, as was the case, he had seller's remorse. Hal did not fully embrace the solution we had agreed upon, so he was having a hard time implementing.

Hal and I met for a private lunch where I guided him through a series of questions intended to elicit an honest and introspective response. I asked if he was lacking trust in anyone on the team, specifically the investment advisor. He indicated that he was not. I asked if he felt the sales price that we established was unfair. His response was to the contrary—Hal thought the sales price was terrific.

So why wasn't he taking action? From my years as an advisor, I suspected that I knew the answer, but I needed Hal to know that I was not pushing my agenda on him, so I continued asking him about the solution. His responses confirmed my suspicion: the problem was discovered at the Clarity Quadrant. In the quiet of his own study, Hal finally confided that he had more battles to fight. His vision of the company had changed since we had last entered the Clarity Quadrant. Hal did not want to sell.

We immediately put all activities regarding sales of the distribution company on hold and began exploring other options. We learned that Jim was content to stay so long as he could be integrated fully into the plumbing division. For five years, Hal and Jim continued to run Two Sons Distributors, making more profits than ever and fully incorporating Jim into the plumbing business.

When implementation feels stiff, difficult, or too complex, you might have buyer's remorse. Either you have not yet found the right solution, or you need to revisit the Clarity Quadrant. The solution is simple: go back to Quadrants One and Two. Do you have clarity? Are your goals defined in clear, specific terms, and are they goals you really want to achieve or goals you think you have to achieve? Do you have a defined plan of action, a solution with concrete steps that, if followed, will result in the achievement of your vision?

The key to implementation is to start acting on the results of your Quadrants One and Two planning, and then to refuse to be diverted from your overall goal. And if you do get diverted, stop, take stock, and get back on the right path to realizing your vision. Solutions, fully explored, vetted with an advisory team, and tied to your overarching goals or vision, should not be overwhelmingly difficult to implement. You should feel excited because all of the issues have been explored. Even if the issues are complex, the path to resolution will be clear because all goals and actions will be outlined. Like a road trip, you might hit detours and have long stretches of road to cover, but your destination will remain clear and desirable if you have successfully navigated through Quadrants One and Two.

Remember: if you do not quit, you have not failed.

KEY POINTS

At some point in the venture, the time comes to stop planning. Once you can answer the following critical questions, you are ready for the Implementation Quadrant:

- *What does the ideal outcome look like?*
- *What is the solution?*
- *How is the solution applicable to the overall vision and goals?*
- *What are the steps necessary to make the solution work?*
- *What can go wrong?*
- *Who are the trusted advisors that must be involved?*
- *Who else must be involved?*
- *How much does it cost to implement?*
- *How much does it cost to sustain?*
- *What must be done to sustain it?*

Pushing against gravity. Breaking out of our habits and routines deprives us of the safety of the familiar and puts us on a path that can be uncomfortable or even scary. Aggravating matters, anytime we try something new, the world's forces try to keep us within the sphere we are already in, throwing obstacles that, like gravity, push us back into our place. To escape from the status quo, we must make the transition into implementation part of the solution. By incorporating a plan to transition into action, we can overcome the barrier and push against gravity.

Just do it. Overcoming procrastination is simple if we identify a small, easy part of the overall task that we can do. By building on momentum, we can start taking larger, more difficult steps once we have catapulted past procrastination and into action.

Using a process. Create a written plan that identifies as many of the details as possible and works to overcome obstacles. The Quadrant Thinking Conductor in the back of this book outlines a general process, serving as a foundation for your specific written plan.

Creating accountability. When expected to meet certain criteria and to be accountable to people, most people will work toward these standards. Many successful people find greater success difficult because they have few people to hold them accountable. When this happens, create artificial accountability, such as a promise to someone, a declaration to a company to make goals, or a rewards system whereby you treat yourself, family, or employees to something fun upon meeting goals. The key is to make sure the stakes are high.

Combating buyer's remorse. If implementation feels stiff, difficult, or too complex, you might have buyer's remorse. Either you have not yet found the right solution, or you need to revisit the Clarity Quadrant. If you are having problems in the Implementation Quadrant, revisit Quadrants One and Two to make sure you have clarity, specific goals you want to accomplish, and a defined plan of action that you understand and feel comfortable implementing.

See the Quadrant Thinking Conductor for help implementing.

QUADRANT FOUR

SUSTAINABILITY

Quadrant Four | SUSTAINABILITY

THE FOURTH QUADRANT IS SUSTAINABILITY, which is the equivalent of a pilot adapting his flight plan to meet unexpected weather conditions. Imagine that your biggest dream is to attend Evel Knievel Days and visit a giant copper mine. The only place to go is, of course, Butte, Montana, hometown of both Evel and a giant copper mine. While awaiting your connecting flight in Denver, you learn that snowstorms in Montana have limited visibility and the runways are so icy that planes cannot land. Flights into Montana are delayed for at least twenty-four hours.

"But I have a plane full of passengers awaiting Evel Knievel Days," says the pilot. "Nothing will stand in the way of my passengers and the celebration of their hero! Indeed, I will embody the spirit of Evel Knievel and land that plane successfully against all odds."

Your pilot insists that the passengers board the plane. He refuses to deviate from his original plan.

Your pilot is a moron.[1] He fails to recognize that sustainability—the practice of continuously reviewing our progress to make sure our vision, plan of attack, and actions are moving us in the direction we want to move in—is an essential part of clarity planning for three reasons:

1. Circumstances change.
2. We learn more about what solutions will and will not enable us to achieve our goals.
3. Our goals change.

---

[1] Butte is the only U.S. city where open containers of alcohol can be legally consumed on the street throughout the entire city. This is probably why the pilot is a moron. He is drunk.

CIRCUMSTANCES CHANGE.

A while back, a television commercial illustrated the consequences of not planning for success. A small group of people running a birthday cake company watch happily as their new online system reflects three birthday cake orders. Their smiles turn to concern as the number jumps from three to three hundred. And in the blink of an eye, three more zeroes are added, bringing the tally to three hundred thousand new cake orders. Their faces show sheer terror.

Whether we like it or not, circumstances have a way of changing. A downturn in the economy ruins our financial projections, an illness sets back our exercise schedule, a change in the tax code makes our estate plan obsolete. We must not become so committed to our solution that we race full steam ahead while ignoring the fact that if we try to fly to Butte, our plane will likely crash into that giant copper mine we so desperately long to see.

WE LEARN MORE ABOUT WHAT SOLUTIONS WILL AND WILL NOT ENABLE US TO ACHIEVE OUR GOALS.

No matter how fastidious we are when designing a solution, no substitute exists for experience.[2] More often than not, we have to adjust our plans as we implement them in order to keep them in line with our goals. This does not mean we should alter our solution just because it turns out to be more difficult than we anticipated. The issue is effectiveness—not ease. If your solution is simply not working, if you are not seeing any results, it is time for a change.

OUR GOALS CHANGE.

Our aims are constantly evolving, either because we find out that we do not want what we think we wanted, or because we have achieved our initial goals and are ready for new, more ambitious ones. To make sure that we are constantly moving toward goals that represent what we are really after and avoid acting out of habit, sustainability is required.

---

2 There is no, "I Can't Believe It's Not Experience!"

Sustainability is important because life does not stand still.[3] Life is a process of learning, growth, and development, where circumstances are always changing. To develop blinders is to ensure that more and more elephants will wander into your room.

What does sustainability consist of? In fact, sustainability is a lot like car maintenance—you simply take in feedback and, if necessary, return to the earlier quadrants to adjust. I may notice that I have been following my exercise and diet plan religiously, but my results have been poor. I would decide to return to Quadrant Two: Solutions and look for new actions that would lead to the achievement of my goals. (On the other hand, if I was not executing my solution, I might want to return to Quadrant One: Clarity to make sure I am emotionally committed to my goal.)

Sustainability, as created by Todd Fithian, is the process of managing and preserving expectations by monitoring the relevance, predictability, and power[4] of a plan. When done well, it answers a few simple questions.

1. *What did I set out to do?*
2. *What happened? Did I achieve the desired results?*
3. *Do I want what happened to continue or change?*

Mechanically, sustainability is a process that evaluates the current state of affairs and measures it against the expected results of your prior planning. It considers the actions that need to be taken to maintain the actions that you have implemented. It also asks the all important question: *What must be done that is undone, and when should the undone be done!*[5]

Quadrant Thinking will always take you to a new beginning whereby you reach a new need for clarity planning. Almost every plan you create will require that you constantly revisit it. Just like you cannot paint your house once and expect the paint to last a lifetime, Quadrant Thinking requires you to consistently review, evaluate, and change your plans.

---

[3] Unless you are a Chicago Cubs' fan.
[4] Fithian uses relevance, predictability, and certainty. With all due respect to Fithian, I think power is stronger.
[5] Peter Piper picked a peck of pickled peppers.

You must not only sustain your techniques, but also review the changes in your life.

THIS QUADRANT ASKS YOU TO CONSIDER THE FOLLOWING QUESTIONS:

- **What do I need to take care of?**
- **What has changed in my life, my business, or my techniques that prompt me to start a new clarity process?**

The casita.

I live in a house that was built in the 1920s to be the casita for a small ranch located in an area that was, at the time, isolated and out of Los Angeles. My house was erected in response to a burgeoning entertainment industry. It was intended for movie stars, celebrities, and high-profile executives or high-stress support staff so they could escape from the masses.

The original structure boasts high-vaulted ceilings in that old adobe way seen in movies that feature the architecture of the old southwest.

Over the years, rooms have been added. I'm given to understand that a past owner was one of the original producers of the *Star Trek* series. He updated all the electrical outlets and installed a Jacuzzi as one did in those days to "Hollywood-up" a residence.

In recent years, my wife and I remodeled the bathrooms, updated the kitchen, added a better air conditioning system, and installed fuel-efficient appliances. In that way, what was built in 1920 or so continues to be pertinent and relevant in the twenty-first century.

Just like my house, any plan needs to be sustained.

QUESTIONS TO ASK DURING
QUADRANT FOUR INCLUDE:

1. **What were the results I was looking for?**
2. **Did I achieve those results?**
3. **If not, what was the problem?**
   - Did the solution not work?
   - Did I fail to implement the solution?
   - Will the solution work if I give the plan more time?
4. **What would it take to achieve the results today?**
   - A change in approach?
   - An entirely new approach?
   - Small tweaks to the approach?

KEEPING IT RELEVANT.

ONCE A LIFETIME AWAY FROM LOS ANGELES, my casita is now located in a bustling suburb of the city. Many of the high-profile executives who in years past would have escaped to this once-isolated part of town now fight traffic and urban sprawl in a part of town they now consider pretty much in the heart of the city.

As a vacation spot in a quaint locale that offers escape from the hustle and bustle, the casita is no longer relevant. It no longer serves its original purpose.

When sustaining a plan, we must ask: *Is this solution still relevant to where I am today?* If the solution no longer works (Quadrant Two) or, if your goals have changed (Quadrant One), you must revise the plan (Quadrant Four) so that your implementation plan (Quadrant Three) will be effective.

| CRITICAL QUESTION |
Is this solution still relevant to where I am and what I want today?

This is what Todd Fithian did when his brother, Scott Fithian, died unexpectedly of pancreatic cancer. Scott was the guiding light of the Legacy Wealth Coaching Program and the Legacy Network, which teaches advisors to use the Planning Horizon,™ a process that serves as the basis for Quadrant Thinking. Their network of financial service firms and professionals give Quadrant Thinking-guided advice so their clients can be happier and more fulfilled.

When Scott died, Todd was forced to take the reins to sustain the company. He, as those around him, had a great deal of trepidation. As capable as Todd is, his peers and subordinates knew he could not run the company the same way Scott ran the company.

Todd used Quadrant Thinking to address this problem. Just like we have improved and added features to my 1920's home, Todd knew he had to take everything good about the existing company and, in an effort to sustain it, change the things that would not work now that the circumstances had changed and new people were living in the casita.

Todd gathered his strong internal team and sought advice from his trusted advisors to plan the transition and move forward. He was sure to honor the concepts of his brother. He paid attention to the history of the business and listened to his partners, but Todd also advocated for fresh approaches that fit better into his operating style.

Up until this point, Todd, Scott, and the Legacy Networks had called the fourth stage "maintenance." But Todd worked with his clients and peers to develop a concept of "sustainability," which speaks more to the crux of this quadrant. In other words, the emergence of this quadrant was a response to a change in a condition within the company that created it!

The Sustainability Quadrant is the lynchpin of everything. It leads us back to the first quadrant and keeps the wheels in motion. Without this quadrant, your plan will eventually come to a standstill. With this quadrant gluing the cyclical process together, you are guaranteed to move one step closer to your goal.

QUESTIONS TO ASK INCLUDE:

1. **Is the solution still relevant to where I am today and what I want today?**
2. **Have the goals changed?**
3. **Have conditions changed in such a way that the solutions will no longer work?**

Sustaining predictability.

ONE OF THE REASONS I AM DEEPLY IN LOVE with Quadrant Thinking is because I can create a link between behavior and outcomes. Understanding what behaviors we need to take on an annual, monthly, or quarterly basis to replicate and sustain desirable results is part of the maintenance plan.

That said, things do not always work the way we first expect them to work. By trying to create a predictable outcome, we begin narrowing down solutions so that we can find the link between behavior and outcomes.

Most planning requires some attention to keep it fresh, current, and in line with your goals. Some planning techniques simply require certain actions to keep the solutions valid and predictable. This might include something as simple as filing forms with the government, paying premiums, or observing protocols to document the legitimacy of a plan.

Or, it may be related to something a little more complex, like the pooling together of assets in a Family Limited Partnership. Very simply stated, family members are rewarded with tax advantages for pooling together their investments or businesses into a Family Limited Partnership. Often times, the oldest generation of a family will contribute one or more assets to an entity, gifting pieces of that entity to their children or grandchildren. So long as there is a business purpose, these arrangements are allowed by the IRS.

However, some families create FLPs and use them for personal affairs. Perhaps Dad withdraws money from the partnership to pay for personal items. Daughter fails to repay advances. Mom distributes money disproportionately to herself or other family members. In failing to observe the formalities of the FLP structure, a family can render this technique totally ineffective, opening themselves up to tax liabilities and audits.

Sustainability is a simple remedy to such issues. A disciplined review of the state of affairs of the Family Limited Partnership should be performed at least annually. As is the case with any business entity, business owners should meet with their advisors to talk about changes in the law and the government's interpretations of the law. The careful attention to sustainability saves businesses and individuals boatloads of money and stops headaches. If you want to make sure things don't suddenly go sideways—that is, if you want to make sure that your results are predictable, sustainability is the answer.

QUESTIONS TO ASK TO MAKE SURE
YOUR PLAN IS PREDICTABLE INCLUDE:

1. **Is this working the way we expected it to be working?**
2. **If not, why?**
   - What did we fail to consider?
   - What unexpected variables came into play, and can we expect these variables to repeat themselves?

HOW SALTY IS YOUR PLAN?
SUSTAINING THE POWER.

I HAVE A FRIEND WHO TELLS THE STORY of one of her first years as a licensed driver. One day, she stopped at a gas station a block away from her father's house, filled her Toyota Corolla with gas, and started to drive away. She made it approximately ten feet before her car stopped.

Frustrated, she walked to her father's house to ask him for help. As she began recounting the story, realization spread across her face.

"I'll be right back," she told her father.

In those days, the diesel fuel pumps were identical to other pumps, and my friend realized she had been daydreaming at the pump. She walked back and confirmed—indeed, she had filled her car with diesel gas, which was far too powerful for her little Corolla.

On the other hand, consider my married clients worth $14,700,000, far above the threshold to avoid paying estate taxes. When they first came to me, they had no plan in place to protect their assets upon death. Instead, their previous planner had encouraged them to write a will designating how they would split their assets upon death. The proper planning, at the least, includes a mechanism that incorporates a bypass trust that saves them about $1,000,000 in estate taxes.

Their existing plan was not powerful enough for their assets.

Because our circumstances change, we want to evaluate the plan's ability to fuel our goals once the plan has been tested. Are we trying to feed a V8 engine with 85-octane fuel? Do we want our food saltier than we did five years ago?

My friend Steve created a business that made him a comfortable living designing websites for small businesses. He had talent for drawing cartoons and often laced his websites with cartoon personas that helped the user "stroll" around the site. His earnings were in the low six figures and he lived well.

We assisted him in installing an employee benefit plan, made the most out of his spending, and created structures that would minimize the risk of double taxation by electing S-Corporation status.

A few years later, his concepts caught the imagination of businesses, and his income sky-rocketed to several million dollars a year. His business was growing by leaps and bounds. There was no stopping Steve!

While he was able to manage the growth, he kept ignoring the huge bite the taxman was taking out of his income. He did not want to spend the time and the money to investigate his options. Instead, he paid close to 40 percent of his new income in taxes. Clearly the solutions implemented in the "before time" did not serve him very well now. If Steve ever consents to a sustainability review, he'll have a six-figure payoff![6]

TO MAKE SURE THE APPROPRIATE AMOUNT OF POWER HAS BEEN ALLOCATED TO YOUR PLAN, ASK:

1. **Is what I'm doing bringing me the most value for the money I am spending?**
2. **Are there things that will make this plan more powerful?**
3. **Is the plan too powerful?**
   - Is the plan creating a ripple effect that is touching unexpected aspects of my life or business that I had not calculated?
   - Is it so successful that we can begin focusing efforts elsewhere and take the foot off the accelerator?

---

6 Steve, are you listening?

M E A S U R I N G   O U T C O M E S .

ONE REASON THAT MANY OF US FAIL is because we do not track our progress very precisely. Part of the key to Rockefeller's success in the oil business was his precise accounting: he always knew whether any element of his business was making money or losing money, and so he could respond accordingly. Today, this has become the standard in the business arena. But how many of us can say we pursue all our goals with that much precision and dedication? The fact is that we need to make our goals and solutions measurable, and then we need to measure them!

The process of Quadrant Thinking is guaranteed to work, so long as you are committed to measuring outcomes and shifting your plan when your goals are not realized. Remember what Thomas Edison said about his search for a material that could act as a filament for his new light bulb: "I have not failed. I've just found 10,000 ways that won't work."

What if Edison, instead of keeping track of each material he tested, simply tried material at random, never writing down the result of the test? Do you think he would have succeeded? Or would he likely have kept going in circles, testing the same useless materials over and over again and finally giving up in frustration?

This represents the need for sustainability, as well as the key to its success. The ability to gain feedback makes it that much more likely that we will accomplish our goals.

**TO MEASURE OUTCOMES, WE ASK
A SERIES OF QUESTIONS THAT START OFF
GENERALLY AND WORK TOWARD SPECIFICITY.
THESE QUESTIONS INCLUDE:**

1. Has the eventual goal been met?
2. What is working?
3. If successful, what are the specific and measurable outcomes that indicate its success?
4. How does the desired outcome (clarity) relate to the present situation (result of implementation)?
5. What is not working?
6. In what ways is the solution not working?
7. Has the goal changed? Or did the solution fail to meet the goal?

LOVING YOUR ELEPHANTS.[7]

WILLIAM AND WILLY (WILLIAM'S SON) run a printing supply business that was a leader in servicing small printers and related business supply needs. William's father, Bill, established the company fifty years ago. The business thrived in the later part of the twentieth century, but the family knew that the company would have to evolve as computer-based digital printing eclipsed the old-style offset printing business.

Several years ago, we proceeded through the quadrants, designing a wise solution that refocused the company's business around digital printing. William and Willy learned the digital printing business inside and out. They researched the market place and made judgments as to what products and suppliers to use.

Two years later and deep into their reserves, William and Willy are still convinced that the conversion to digital format is the right move, but things are not working as they had anticipated. Their sales are not improving as they had hoped.

Their challenge now is to determine how to improve sales while still embracing the newer methods of printing. This is the elephant they must address, and in doing so, Willy and William know they will turn their disappointing results into a successful solution.

Facing the elephants forces you to grow. If you cut and run at the first sign of trouble, you will never move past your current situation. For this reason, many of my clients have come to love the presence of elephants. It

---

[7] In a totally non-creepy way.

challenges them to kick, scream, and make scrambled eggs from those that have been broken. And in doing so, they become bigger, stronger, and more powerful.

The moral: welcome elephants into your home. Shower them with affection. Get to know them. Ask them where they came from and why they are important. And then eat them, one bite at a time.

KEY POINTS

Similar to a pilot who must adjust his flight plan to meet unexpected weather conditions, you must sustain your plan once it has been implemented by considering two questions:

- *What do I need to take care of?*
- *What has changed in my life, my business, or my techniques that prompt me to start a new clarity process?*

The casita. Just like a house, a plan must be maintained. Sustaining plans is critical for three reasons: 1) Circumstances change; 2) We learn more about the solutions we have chosen to achieve our goals; and 3) Our goals change. To make sure your plan is still relevant, ask:

1. *What were the results I was looking for?*
2. *Did I achieve those results?*
3. *If not, what was the problem?*
   - *Did the solution not work?*
   - *Did I fail to implement the solution?*
   - *Will the solution work if I give the plan more time?*
4. *What would it take to achieve the results today?*
   - *A change in approach?*
   - *An entirely new approach?*
   - *Small tweaks to the approach?*

Keeping it relevant. When sustaining a plan, ask if the solution is still relevant. If the solution no longer works, or if your goals have changed, you must revise the plan. Questions to make sure your plan is still relevant include:

- *Is the solution still relevant to where I am today and what I want today?*
- *Have the goals changed?*
- *Have conditions changed in such a way that the solutions will no longer work?*

Sustaining predictability. Be sure that you can create a link between behavior and outcome. Understand the behaviors that must be taken annually, monthly, or quarterly to replicate and sustain desired results. Be sure to ask:

- *Is this working the way we expected it to be working?*
- *If not, why? What did we fail to consider? What unexpected variables came into play, and can we expect these variables to repeat themselves?*

How salty is your plan? Sustaining the power. Because our circumstances change, we want to evaluate their ability to fuel our goals once solutions have been tested. To make sure the appropriate amount of power has been allocated to your plan, ask:

- *Is what I'm doing bringing me the most value for the money I am spending?*
- *Are there things that will make this plan more powerful?*
- *Is the plan too powerful? Is the plan creating a ripple effect that is touching unexpected aspects of my life or business that I had not calculated? Is it so successful that we can begin focusing efforts elsewhere and take the foot off the acceleration?*

Measuring outcomes. Quadrant Thinking is guaranteed to work, so long as you are committed to measuring outcomes and shifting your plan when goals are not realized. The ability to gain feedback makes it that much more likely that we will accomplish our goals. To measure outcomes, ask a series of questions:

- *Has the eventual goal been met?*
- *What is working?*
- *If successful, what are the specific and measurable outcomes that indicate a plan's success?*
- *How does the desired outcome relate to the present situation?*
- *What is not working?*
- *In what ways is the solution not working?*
- *Has the goal changed? Or did the solution fail to meet the goal?*

Loving your elephants. Facing your elephants forces you to grow. If you cut and run at the first sign of trouble, you will never move past your current situation. For this reason, you might come to love the presence of elephants. They challenge you to kick, scream, and make scrambled eggs from those that have been broken. And in doing so, you will become bigger, stronger, and more powerful. The moral of the story: welcome elephants into your home. Shower them with affection. Get to know them. Ask them where they came from and why they are important. And then eat them, one bite at a time.

THE QUADRANT THINKING CONDUCTOR

The Quadrant Thinking Conductor is a tool that creates a jumping off point for people who would like to use Quadrant Thinking to solve problems, identify elephants, and move toward desired goals. The Conductor is most successful when used with the guidance of a team of trusted advisors.

The Quadrant Thinking Conductor

The Quadrant Thinking Conductor
Quadrant One | CLARITY

THE GOAL OF THE CLARITY QUADRANT is to identify your most important life desires and goals, take advantage of opportunities, and discover your elephants, which might be:

1. Unmet needs or dreams
2. Problems

SECTION A—VALUES

Identify the values related to your unmet need, vision, or problem. List these values below. You might ask:

- What are the values most meaningful to me?
- What makes me proud?
- Who are the people most important to me?
- What accomplishments are important to me?

1. _____
2. _____
3. _____
4. _____
5. _____
6. _____
7. _____
8. _____
9. _____
10. _____
11. _____
12. _____
13. _____
14. _____
15. _____
16. _____
17. _____
18. _____
19. _____
20. _____

SECTION B—THE SWOT ANALYSIS

Complete a SWOT Analysis to determine your Strengths, Weaknesses, Opportunities, and Threats.

- What are my **strengths**? What attributes, resources, and skills do I have? In what activities do I feel most confident?

- What are my internal **weaknesses**? What keeps me awake at night? What are the things that would need to be eliminated in order for me to feel safe? What skills do I lack that interfere with my values? What attributes of mine might present obstacles to being happy?

- What are the **opportunities** I have? What external conditions might help me realize and affirm my values?

- What about the external **threats**? Are there outside conditions that might hinder achievement of my objective?

Threats	Opportunities	Weaknesses	Strengths

SECTION C—IDENTIFYING THE DESIRED RESULT

Start by asking: *What does the ideal outcome look like?* This "outcome" might be as complex as a life vision or business endeavor or as simple as losing weight or learning a new skill. List the answer(s) to this question below. These are the criteria by which you will judge the efficacy of your solutions. Be sure they are SMART (Specific, Measurable, Actionable, Relevant and Time-Bounded).

1. _____

2. _____

3. _____

4. _____

5. _____

6. _____

7. _____

8. _____

9. _____

10. _____

If you need to find clarity to resolve a problem, you should ask: *What is the problem?* As you learned from the Decision Swamp, some problems are actually symptoms. Take time to determine whether your problem is an actual problem or a perceived problem that is actually a symptom of another problem.

Use the following worksheet to discover whether the problem is perceived or actual.

Assume for a moment that the problem as you know it is actually the problem and not the symptom of another problem.

List your problem: _____

_____

_____

_____

What solutions have you considered? _____

_____

_____

_____

_____

_____

_____

_____

_____

Why have these solutions failed? _____

_____

_____

_____

_____

_____

Now consider that the problem you listed above is actually a symptom of a larger problem. Place it in the appropriate space below.

Actual problem: _____

_____

Symptom: _____

_____

With your advisors, begin exploring what the actual problem might be. Ask:

- What is causing the symptom?

_____

- Are there truths that I am ignoring?

_____

_____

_____

- How do I contribute to the symptom?

_____

_____

_____

SECTION D—MILESTONES

Identify the milestones necessary for success, as well as the resources necessary to achieve these milestones. List these on the following page.

Resources															

Milestones															

SECTION E—SAYING HELLO TO THE ELEPHANT

Finally, before moving to Quadrant Two, list the elephant(s) you discovered in the Clarity Quadrant:

_____

_____

_____

_____

_____

_____

_____

_____

_____

_____

_____

_____

_____

The Quadrant Thinking Conductor
QUADRANT TWO | SOLUTIONS

THE GOAL OF THE SOLUTIONS QUADRANT is to synthesize the information learned from the Clarity Quadrant to create a solution that meets all objectives and is powerful, predictable, and relevant.

Often, the clarity you achieved in the first quadrant will narrow your choices to an obvious solution.

SECTION A—RESOURCES

Ask what resources are necessary to make the unmet need or dream come to fruition/the problem go away. These resources might be people, strategies, or money. List this information below:

1. _____

2. _____

3. _____

4. _____

5. _____

6. _____

7. _____

8. _____

9. _____

10. _____

11. _____

12. _____

My trusted advisor team includes:

Role	Trusted Advisor Score[1]	Name of Advisor

[1]$\dfrac{C+R+I}{S}$ = TA SCORE

SECTION B—OBSTACLES

Explain the obstacles you will likely meet, and how you will overcome them.

1. _____

   a. _____

   b. _____

   c. _____

2. _____

   a. _____

   b. _____

   c. _____

3. _____

   a. _____

   b. _____

   c. _____

4. _____

   a. _____

   b. _____

   c. _____

5. _____

   a. _____

   b. _____

   c. _____

6. _____

   a. _____

   b. _____

   c. _____

7.

    a.

    b.

    c.

8.

    a.

    b.

    c.

9.

    a.

    b.

    c.

10.

    a.

    b.

    c.

SECTION C—SOLUTIONS SET

Considering all of the information you have collected, design your solution, being sure that it answers these questions:

1. What is the easy first step I will take to implement this plan?

2. How have I made all the stepping stones and milestones Specific, Measurable, Actionable, Relevant, and Time-Bounded? (See following page.)

3. How can I incorporate overcoming the obstacles I discovered in the Clarity Quadrant into my plan for success?

4. Have I considered the elements that will be necessary to complete a sustainability review (Quadrant 4)?

   ☐ Yes
   ☐ No

5. On the following page identify each step. Have you incorporated plans to overcome obstacles into this timeline?

   ☐ Yes
   ☐ No

Stepping Stones/Milestones	Resources	Date of Implementation

SECTION D—EATING THE ELEPHANT ONE BITE AT A TIME

If you and your advisors have discovered a solution set, ask:

- Do I completely understand the solution set that is being proposed?

  ☐ Yes
  ☐ No

- What is the solution set?

  _____

  _____

  _____

  _____

- How is it applicable to my SWOT?

  _____

  _____

  _____

- Why does it work?

  _____

  _____

- What can go wrong?

  _____

  _____

  _____

- Who must be involved?

- How much does it cost to implement?

- How must does it cost to sustain?

- What must be done to sustain it?

- Do the components of the solution set directly relate to the elephant discovered in the Clarity Quadrant? Do they follow the commander's intent?

☐ Yes
☐ No

- Does the solution set affirm the values I listed in the Clarity section?

☐ Yes
☐ No

*If you cannot answer these questions, or if you answer **no** to any of these questions, return to Quadrant One to find clarity or Quadrant Two for a more appropriate solution.*

The Quadrant Thinking Conductor
Quadrant Three: Implementation

In this quadrant, you will stop planning and start acting. In this quadrant, it is important that you keep small, manageable steps, and that you keep yourself accountable.

SECTION A—ACCOUNTABILITY

In the spaces that follow list the steps that will be a challenge to implement, as well as the deadline and the ways in which you will keep yourself accountable.

Goal	Date to Be Completed	Accountability Item

The Quadrant Thinking Conductor
QUADRANT FOUR: SUSTAINABILITY

AFTER A DECENT PERIOD OF IMPLEMENTATION and considering the desired results you collected in the Clarity Quadrant, evaluate the efficacy of your solution set by measuring whether your outcomes have eliminated threats, overcome weaknesses, capitalized on opportunities, or preserved and supported your strengths.

SECTION A—DESIRED RESULTS

List the desired anticipated result(s) in the space provided below:

1. _____

2. _____

3. _____

4. _____

5. _____

6. _____

7. _____

8. _____

9. _____

10. _____

11. _____

12. _____

13. _____

SECTION B—EVALUATING RESULTS

With the help of your trusted advisor team, review your results, goals, and solutions.

- What were the results you were looking for?

- Has the eventual goal been met?

☐ Yes
☐ No

If not, what was the problem?

- Did the solution fail to work? (If yes, return to Quadrant Two.)

☐ Yes
☐ No

- Did you fail to implement the solution? (If yes, return to Quadrant One to make sure you are committed to the goal. If you are, return to Quadrant Two to make sure the solution resonates with your values.)

☐ Yes
☐ No

- Will the solution work if you give the plan more time? (If so, modify the timeline in Quadrant Two accordingly, and schedule your next sustainability review.)

  ☐ Yes
  ☐ No

- Is the goal still relevant to where you are today and what you want today? (If not, return to Quadrant One.)

  ☐ Yes
  ☐ No

- Have conditions changed in such a way that the solutions will no longer work? (If so, return to Quadrant Two.)

  ☐ Yes
  ☐ No

- What unexpected variables came into play, and can you expect these variables to repeat themselves? (If so, return to Quadrant Two.)

  ☐ Yes
  ☐ No

- Are the people on your team committed to the solution? (If not, select a new group of advisors, or revisit the Solutions Quadrant to draft a solution everyone can commit to.)

  ☐ Yes
  ☐ No

- What would it take to achieve the results today?
  A change in approach? (If yes, return to Quadrant Two.)

  ☐ Yes
  ☐ No

- An entirely new approach? (If yes, return to Quadrant Two.)

  ☐ Yes
  ☐ No

- Small tweaks to the approach? (If yes, return to Quadrant Two.)

  ☐ Yes
  ☐ No

If the solutions were effective, answer the following questions:

- Is the solution still relevant to where you are today and what you want today? (If no, return to Quadrant One.)

  ☐ Yes
  ☐ No

- Have the goals changed? (If yes, return to Quadrant One.)

  ☐ Yes
  ☐ No

- Is what you are doing bringing you the most value for the money you are spending? (If not, return to Quadrant Two to develop a more efficient solution.)

  ☐ Yes
  ☐ No

- Are the people on your team committed to the solution? (If not, select a new group of advisors, or revisit the Solutions Quadrant to draft a solution everyone can commit to.)

☐ Yes
☐ No

- What are the things that are working, and what needs to change?

_____

_____

_____

- Are there things that will make this plan more powerful?

_____

_____

_____

Finally, and regardless of whether the solution was successful, answer these questions:

- What do you need to take care of?

_____

_____

_____

_____

_____

_____

- What has changed in your life, your business, or your techniques that prompt you to start a new clarity process?

- Was there anything you failed to consider?

REFERENCES

The Trusted Advisor by David H. Maister, Charles H. Green, and Robert M. Galford

A Whole New Mind by Daniel H. Pink

Blue Ocean Strategy by W. Chan Kim and Renée Mauborgne

The Conative Connection by Kathy Kolbe

Powered by Instinct by Kathy Kolbe

Pure Instinct by Kathy Kolbe

Unique Ability by Dan Sullivan, Catherine Nomura, Julia Waller, and Shannon Waller

The E-Myth Revisited by Michael E. Gerber

Values-Based Estate Planning by Scott C. Fithian

Made to Stick by Chip and Dan Heath

The Ultimate Gift by Jim Stovall

Your Life by Design by Curtis Estes

Managing in the 21st Century by Eric W. Swenson

Sell the Feeling by Larry Pinci and Phil Glosserman

www.HolaElefante.com